FLAVOURS FROM INDIA

Thangam E. Philip, former Principal of the Institute of Hotel Management, Catering and Applied Nutrition Bombay, has been actively involved in hotel and catering education in India since its inception. Her work has also included books, regular features in journals, broadcasts on nutrition, membership of important national committees concerned with nutritional plans and problems, and papers given at several international and FAO conferences. In 1976 she was awarded the FAO's 'Ceres' medal, in honour of her outstanding work in nutrition.

Other Books by Thangam Philip

Modern Cookery for Teaching and the Trade Vol. 1
Modern Cookery for Teaching and the Trade Vol. 2
Thangam Philip Book of Baking

FLAVOURS FROM INDIA

Thangam E. Philip

Illustrations by
Anant Kulkarni

Disha Books

Disha Books
An imprint of Orient Longman Limited

ORIENT LONGMAN LIMITED

Registered Office:
3-6-272 Himayatnagar, Hyderabad 500 029 (A.P.) INDIA

Other Offices:
Kamani Marg, Ballard Estate, Bombay 400 038
17 Chittaranjan Avenue, Calcutta 700 072
160 Anna Salai, Madras 600 002
1/24 Asaf Ali Road, New Delhi 110 002
80/1 Mahatma Gandhi Road, Bangalore 560 001
365 Shahid Nagar, Bhubaneshwar 751 007
41/316 'Gour Mohan', Ambady Lane, Chittoor Road, Cochin 682 011
S.C. Goswami Road, Panbazar, Guwahati 781 001
3-6-272 Himayatnagar, Hyderabad 500 029
28/31, 15 Ashok Marg, Lucknow 226 001
City Centre Ashok, Govind Mitra Road, Patna 800 004

Published in 1993 as a Disha Book

© Orient Longman Limited, 1993
Reprinted 1996
ISBN 81 250 0817 9

Typeset at Phoenix Phototype Setters, 708 Dalamal Tower,
Bombay 400 021

Printed in India at Shantdurga Printers Pvt. Ltd., Sion,
Bombay 400 022.

Published by Orient Longman Ltd., Kamani Marg, Ballard Estate,
Bombay 400 038.

CONTENTS

INTRODUCTION	1
CEREALS	15
DALS	29
VEGETABLES	34
EGGS	50
FISH	53
MEAT	62
POULTRY	76
SWEETS	85
SNACKS	96
PICKLES	112
INDEX OF RECIPES AND MAIN INGREDIENTS	118

INTRODUCTION

Indian food, like food in other parts of the world, has been influenced by the geography, history, religion, customs, economics and agriculture of the land. In this vast country, food flavours and food habits vary from region to region. However, over the centuries certain influences have had a major and lasting impact on Indian cuisine. For example, the concept of Ahimsa (non-violence) preached by religions like Buddhism and Jainism has resulted in a distinct and unique vegetarian cuisine. This is one of the reasons why the vegetarian repertoire in India is extensive.

While there are as many varieties of food as there are dialects in our country, there is a certain uniformity in the diversity. All Indian food is spicy—the quantum and nature of spices varying from region to region. Strange as it may seem, spices such as cardamom, cloves, cinnamon, nutmeg and pepper although grown in the south of India, are more generously used in the cuisine of the north. This may be attributed to the influence of the Moghul rule during which time more expensive, rare and rich commodities such as nuts, spices, milk and milk products were used liberally in North Indian cooking. In all types of Indian food the meal is built around one, or more than one, cereal: rice in South India and Bengal, wheat in North India and wheat or millet, in addition to rice, in Western India.

Food is eaten with one's hands. There is no such thing as successive courses, as found in Western meals; the same plate/thali/leaf is used for the entire meal. Throughout India, along with the staple cereal is served one dal or pulse dish, a vegetable, curd (yoghurt) or curd preparation, pickle, pappads and if the meal is non-vegetarian, meat/chicken/fish as an accompaniment. The cooking medium varies; ghee is used more prolifically in the North, mustard oil to a lesser degree; mustard oil in Bengal; til or sesame seed oil in Andhra Pradesh and Tamil Nadu; coconut oil in Kerala and Karnataka; peanut oil in Western India. Ghee, however, has the pride of place in all Indian cuisine. Milk sweets are popular and served on festivals, anniversaries, etc. and are considered auspicious in all regions, and *paan* (betel leaf and nuts) is generally eaten after meals.

Regional cuisine is influenced by the staple cereal available in the area. Wheat is the main crop of North India and with plenty of pasture land available in this region, there is an abundance of milk from cattle. Punjabi food basically consists of chapaties, parathas, stuffed parathas, etc., served with milk or milk products such as curd, butter or paneer. Sometimes corn bread (*makai di roti*) replaces wheat chapaties. Lentils in one form or another are used in plenty, while spinach and mustard leaves (*sarason ka saag*) are two favourite leafy vegetables. More of the so called 'English' vegetables are used in the North as they can be grown there in the winter months. Salads are served

INTRODUCTION 3

without dressings. The tandoori chicken, different types of kababs, nans and tandoori roti, linked with Punjabi food and popularised universally by commercial food outlets, are dishes adapted from the cuisine of the nomadic tribes who came over to India looking for pasturelands.

Sweet dishes such as hulwas and kheers made with vegetables like carrot, beetroot, gourd and pumpkin and cooked with milk, ghee and sugar are unique to Punjab, with the carrot hulwa reigning supreme.

There is a lavish use of gramflour (*besan*), buttermilk and ghee in the vegetarian food of Uttar Pradesh. Wheat is the staple food with rice served sparingly. The non-vegetarian food of Lucknow, however, is typical of the Moghul influence, rich in spices, nuts, cream, buttermilk, curd, *mawa* and saffron, resplendent of the glory that once was.

Some of the former princely states of India can truly boast of the 'haute cuisine' of our country. The food of the former state of Rampur is one such example. These states, ruled by nawabs, gave India some great dishes, rich in taste and ingredients, such as *masalum raan, sag gosht, paya, nahari, kichada/ haleem, burani, dam ka murgh, lukmi,* a great variety of *kababs, dalcha, bagara baingan, mirchi ka salan, tomato kut, andeki piyosi, dum ka pooran, double ka meetha,* etc. Great care was taken in the presentation of the food as in the preparation. Some influence of French and Continental cooking can also be found in a few dishes.

The common man's food in Rajasthan is simple—mostly *bajre ki roti* or *jowar ki roti* with *saag* or *mooli bhaji*, lassi and pickle—as the parched and dry land yields little vegetation and as the Rajasthanis have, by tradition, been nomadic. In the palaces of Jaipur and the houses of the élite, however, one finds a rich non-vegetarian cuisine using mostly game meat, as the Rajputs are masters in the art of shikar.

The neighbouring state of Gujarat is essentially vegetarian. Here again the peasant food consists of *bajra* or *jowar rotlo* or *bhakri* eaten with locally grown vegetables such as brinjal, a variety of beans and gourds, fenugreek leaves, lentils and milk. Pappad is a great favourite and every house prepares its own variety. The more urbanised Gujarati normally eats wafer thin chapaties or delightfully light puris with *shak* (vegetable). In Gujarat as well as in Maharashtra, the sweet dish is served along with the main meal and eaten with puris. When rice is brought to the table in Gujarat, it is an indication that the meal is nearly over. There is a blend of both the sweet and the spicy in Gujarati and Maharashtrian food.

To the Bengali the preparation of food is a ritual. Even the purchase of ingredients required for cooking is turned into a fine art. Fish is selected for its flavour and freshness—Hilsa being a hot favourite and Rohu or carp a good second—and vegetables for their freshness, juiciness, shape, colour and texture. The art of cutting fish and vegetables (different sizes and thicknesses for each dish) is well developed. Rice milled from the short round parboiled Bengal grain, is the staple food, generally served plain boiled. Refined flour rather than wholemeal flour is used to prepare luchi —a thin delicate puri—and Dhakai parathas are served occasionally. Many of the indigenous vegetables are used in Bengali recipes like *shukto, bajja, dalna, charchari, niramish jhal* etc. *Macher jhol, doi mach* and *sarsobate mach*, which are some of the more popular fish dishes, are quite distinct in flavour. The delicious milk sweets of Bengal reflect an abundant availability of milk. Cow's milk is used for milk sweets and buffalo milk for the rich sweet curd, *mishti doi*.

As in most rice-eating states, rice is eaten thrice a day by the average person in Orissa. For breakfast rice, cooked the previous night and soaked in water and salt, is eaten with salted mangoes squeezed into it. Since the land is very fertile, irrigated by various rivers and natural springs, every village has natural ponds to breed fish. Like the Bengali, the Oriya does not relish saltwater fish. *Chanchoda*, a dry dish made of large fish heads, vegetables and spices is a must in a wedding meal. The Oriya has a penchant for mixing different ingredients like fish and vegetables, lentils and vegetables etc. As the Marathas ruled Orissa at one time, a certain Maratha influence is seen in a few dishes, especially in the sweets. *Chena-podo-ptha*, a paneer dish baked in an earthen vessel heated by surrounding it with burning cowdung, is typical to Orissa.

Sikkim, the border state of India, is a mountainous region. The hill people generally eat simple food, but enjoy venison, beef, pork and fish from the mountain streams. These meats are eaten with boiled rice or maize and rice cooked together and washed down with *chang*, the liquor made from maize or millet. Special dishes such as *gyakhog* (a variety of meat and fish cooked between layers of river/lake weeds in metal vessels made of a copper and brass alloy) are delicacies.

A favourite dish of the Lepchas of Sikkim is the bamboo fish, delicately flavoured and cooked in a bamboo stem surrounded by burning charcoal. It is served in the split bamboo itself. *Momos* and some of the snacks found in Sikkim are influenced by the cuisine of Tibet.

Bihar is divided by the river Ganga into two areas of distinct cultures. Culturally influenced by Bengal and Uttar Pradesh, and the nawabs who once ruled the state, food in this state reflects a mix of these influences. Typical to North Bihar is the *chura* or beaten rice (*poha*) which is the staple diet. It is eaten in large quantities with thick curd, a speciality of this area, or with milk and jaggery or sugar, and features on everyday, as well as festive, menus. Wheat is the staple grain of south Bihar, and *sattu* (Bengal gram) is mixed with wheat to make the well known *litti* balls. Baked traditionally in a cowdung fire, the spiced balls are filled with ghee through a hole made in them by the thumb, and eaten with either hot green or red chilli chutney or a *baingan* (brinjal) *bhurta*. While *chura* preparations are easy to digest, one needs a strong constitution for *litti*. Other dishes include rice dumplings filled with masoor dal paste or with jaggery and a kind of oil seed known as *teesi*. The dumplings, boiled in water, are eaten plain if sweet or with hot green or red chilli chutney, if savoury.

Goa, a coastal state, revels in its seafood dishes, but is also famous for its *pork vindaloo, sorpotel,* etc. Goan food is an exotic blend of the state's Portuguese heritage and indigenous flavour. The cuisine of Goa is built around rice (boiled plain), coconut and fish. The Goan has his first main meal at 9 or 10 a.m.—eating rice congee with a little pickle or *kalchi kori* (yesterday's curry)—and ends the day with a rice and fish curry meal. Breakfast amongst average Goans is just tea with a toddy-leavened bread. Lunch is generally a fish curry and plain boiled, partially milled, parboiled rice. Vegetables are not very important in the Goan diet. Sometimes a meat dish such as *meat baffat* or *pork vindaloo* is served at teatime and dinner follows more or less the same pattern as lunch. It is only on festive occasions that dishes like chicken *chacouti*, roast suckling pig, etc. are included. *Feni,* a liquor distilled from cashewfruit (grown abundantly in Goa), or else palm toddy, is the most popular drink and is consumed in plenty.

The élite of Goa are more selective in their eating habits. They normally have a breakfast of Goan sausages, scrambled eggs and local bread, a lunch of boiled rice with stuffed crab or king fish (*rechado*), a vegetable caldeen or foogath and a mutton or chicken *chacouti.* Dinner may start with a soup, followed by roast pork marinaded in a blend of spices and toddy/vinegar and eaten with bread or rice. Lunch and dinner may end with *bibinca* (a layered baked custard made with coconut milk, eggs, flour and sugar) or *dos de grao* or *dodol* reflecting the Portuguese influence more patently.

The higher echelons of the hierarchy of Tamil Hindus are predominantly vegetarian. Though the food is basically very simple, nowhere in the world can one find such a variety of vegetarian dishes as in Tamil Nadu. The *idli, dosa, oothappam, uppuma, sambar* and *rasam* popularised all over India by the South Indian restaurants constitutes only a microcosm of the vast repertoire. Despite this, there is a large population of non-vegetarians in Tamil Nadu. In fact, the word 'curry' (meat or fish in a gravy) is of Tamil origin, although to the Brahmin of Tamil Nadu the curry is a dry vegetable dish. The variety of non-vegetarian dishes available, however, is limited. Rice is the main staple. In areas where there is an abundance of water, paddy sugarcane and bananas dominate the cuisine. In dry areas where only millets like Ragi and some gram are grown, these form the base.

The culinary scene in Karnataka is similar to that of Tamil Nadu, except in coastal areas such as Mangalore and Karwar, where fish dishes prevail. The spices vary somewhat but basically the everyday dishes are the same. Some special dishes are the outcome of the patronage of the royal household of Mysore and the festivals of Karnataka. The cuisine of Mangalore, however, is distinct, varied and interesting.

As Andhra Pradesh is the rice bowl of India, rice is the staple food in that state, served plain, or else flavoured as in some of the mouthwatering biryanis. The vegetarian food of Andhra Pradesh is akin to the vegetarian food of Tamil Nadu and Karnataka. *Chitrannam* (lime rice), til rice, *pulihore* (tamarind rice) are dishes popular in all these states. *Sambar, rasam* and vegetable preparations, and *idli, dosa* etc, are also common. Andhra chillies, known for their pungency, are a commercial crop of the state. *Avakkai,* the hot mango pickle of Andhra, is a necessary adjunct to its food. Ghee is served with hot rice and *sambar,* and is also used for *baghar* (the tempering of food). Til oil is used for cooking and for making pickles. Andhra is also famous for its *gongura* (rosella) *pachadi*—a form of cooked green chutney served with hot boiled rice and ghee. Lake fish is used more than sea fish in fish dishes such as *machli ka salan, machli ka kaitya* etc.

Kerala has three distinct cuisines, apart from variations within the theme. These are the Hindu, the Syrian Christian and the Muslim cuisines. The Chakiyars—one of the subcastes of the Namboodiri Brahmins—are the repositories of the authentic Kerala Hindu cuisine, and still prepare the food in the temples according to the Shastras. For example, the 'Shatrass' or six flavours—sweet, sour, pungent, salty, bitter and astringent—must be present in each meal. So should foods requiring the different textures for biting, drinking, relishing (licking) and chewing. Food has thus evolved to meet the shastrik requirements. Dishes like *parippu, erussery, puliserry, pachadi, kitchadi, kalam, colan, thoran, thiyyal, upperi, meahukuperatti, ingipuli* etc. are typical. The better-known dish, *avial,* is really an innovation. A variety of *payasams* made with rice, milk and sugar, or roasted grams, coconut milk and molasses, or jackfruit, coconut and molasses are served as a sweet just prior to eating curd and rice. Boiled, parboiled and hand-pounded rice is the staple, although more and more of milled and polished rice is being eaten today. All the other dishes are accompaniments to rice.

The Syrian Christian cuisine, besides borrowing heavily from the Hindu cuisine, has also been influenced by the Syrian ancestors, Dutch or Portuguese, as well as by the British missionaries. *Meen vivichathu*, a hot chilli, red curry, is just fish cooked with roasted and ground red chillies (a modicum of turmeric, coriander, red onion and garlic is ground with the red chillies) and balanced with *kudampuli*, a fleshier version of the cocum found in the Konkan area. *Kudampuli* is used in most of the fish dishes. It not only balances the hot, sour, salt flavour but also acts as an antiseptic and as an anti-allergent. Coconut oil is used as the cooking medium especially for fish, *avial* etc. Coconut, grated, ground or in the form of milk extract, is used in most of the preparations.

Hoppers or griddle cakes edged with a thin lace border made from rice flour, toddy and coconut milk, and rice *puttu* —moist rice flour mixed with grated coconut and steamed in bamboos — are the common breakfast dishes besides rice congee. A modified stew of chicken or duck or meat, using coconut milk and onion and spices like green chillies and ginger is served with the griddle cake (*palappam*: hopper). A dried beef dish (*irachy olathiyathu*) which is served at practically all the meals, may accompany the rice *puttu*. Boiled breadfruit, yam, tapioca and jackfruit or tapioca and raw jackfruit cooked with coconut are also served with a coconut or chilli chutney for breakfast, during season, as also steamed ripe Kerala bananas. Interestingly enough, there is a great similarity between the Syrian Christian food of Kerala and the Sinhalese food of Sri Lanka.

The Muslims in Kerala, known as the Moplahs, have a cuisine influenced by Arab food. The Moplahs are descendants of intermarriage between Arab traders and local women, and in the cuisine the blend is patent. Although rice and coconut and coconut oil are the base, there are quite a few wheat dishes as well. While rice flour is used for the famous *pattiri* or the

Moplah chapati, it may be an adaptation. Wheat is used to prepare a type of pulao and even boiled and eaten instead of rice. The *neichoru* (ghee rice) could be a type of pilaff of the Middle East. The chicken and mutton biryanis have a Moghul overtone.

Maharashtrian cuisine is known for its simplicity. By and large Maharashtrians are non-vegetarians except for the Brahmin groups. The coastal communities have a wide range of seafoods cooked in plenty of coconut milk or in oil. Their basic meals consist of rice as well as puris and chapaties of wheat, *bhakris* of jowar or bajri. Dals are a must and sprouted dals are very popular. A salad of broken or ground, roasted peanuts, and chopped vegetables like cucumber or cabbage and one or two dry vegetables, mostly potatoes with a locally grown vegetable, such as brinjal, gawar, tindli, papdi etc. are usually served with every meal. Pickle, lime and a curd dish or curd accompany the food. On festive occasions a sweet such as *jilebi*, *shrikhand* or *puranpoli* may be served. During the mango season, *aamras*, served with puris or chapaties, is very popular. The predominant flavours are sweet and sour, with jaggery and tamarind being the most commonly used ingredient for getting the above flavours in the meal. The Maharashtrian starts his meal with rice, *varan* (a semi-liquid dal) and ghee followed by wheat or jowar bread, and concludes it with rice and curd. *Ussals* made out of a variety of sprouted pulses are unique. *Amtis* (liquid dal preparations with different temperings and vegetables) are served with rice or chapaties.

Bombay, offers many interesting cuisines belonging to a multitude of cultures. Besides the Maharashtrian,

12 INTRODUCTION

Gujarati and Udipi (from Karnataka) there are the East Indian, the Parsi and the Bohra cuisines, all indigenous to Bombay. While borrowing from one another, these cuisines have maintained an identity of their own. East Indian food is a synergy of many influences, the Maharashtrian, the Portuguese, the Dutch, the British and may be even the Muslim.

The Parsis, who imbibed the habits and customs of the host country when they migrated to India from Iran about 1,300 years ago, adopted many of the local dietary patterns, but as "gourmets par excellence" they have also been influenced by the cuisines of many nations. The Parsis are largely non-vegetarian in their food preferences. By borrowing from the Iranian, Gujarati and European cuisines, they have come up with some tantalising dishes like their well-known mutton/chicken pulao, *dhansak, machhi no sas, patra ni machhi, kid ghosh, sali ma murghi* and a wide range of egg dishes. The vegetables served with their food are the local ones like papdi, gavar, etc. Garlic, ginger and onions are used liberally.

A cuisine popular with the people of Bombay is that of the Bohras. Their delicious and distinctive dishes have been inspired both by the local cuisine of the converts to Islam, primarily Gujarati, and perhaps Malwas, Rajputs and Marathas, and by the culinary practices of Egypt, Iraq, Syria and Iran. The blend has created a variety of gourmet foods. The practice of eating along with several other people from a common thali is quite distinctive to the Bohra community; it constitutes a part of their religious injunctions and signifies brotherhood. Usually about eight or nine people sit around a large thali laden with food. The meal starts with a pinch of salt which is offered to and consumed by all in token of the equality of all men. On festive occasions this is followed by rice cooked in milk and sweetened. A mix of sweet and savoury dishes follows. The savoury dishes are mostly non-vegetarian, containing beef, mutton or chicken.

The *sheer khurma,* one of the favourite Bohra sweets, highlights the culinary route taken by the Arabs to the East. This dessert which in its original form consists of dates mixed with milk from Iran and dry fruits and nuts from Afghanistan is modified in India by the addition of fried semia and caramelised sugar.

There is no end to the variety of Indian food, which is also one of the most imaginative and nutritious cuisines in the world.

CEREALS

1. Boiled Rice

Rice	500 gm.	Water	1 litre
Salt	10 gm.		

1. Wash and soak rice. 2 Bring water to the boil. 3. Add rice and salt and simmer. 4. Cook till rice is tender and water has evaporated.

Serves 4.

Culinary Cue: Cooking rice in large quantities of water and throwing away the liquor is a wasteful practice, since the water in which rice has been boiled contains a lot of vitamins and minerals. Rice should be boiled by the absorption method, where rice is added to hot water of approximately twice its volume and allowed to cook gently after it has come to the boiling point once.

2. Yellow Rice

Pulao rice	500 gm.	Cloves	
Fat	50 gm.	Cinnamon	2 gm.
Onions	115 gm.	Bay leaf	each
Turmeric	a pinch	Cardamoms	
Salt	to taste	Badyani (star anise)	
Water or stock	1 litre		

1. Clean, wash and soak rice. 2. Slice onions. 3. Heat fat. Fry sliced onions. Remove. 4. Fry spices. Add rice and fry. 5. Add turmeric dissolved in a little water; stir well. 6. Add hot water or stock in the proportion 1:2 and salt. 7. To finish, when rice is cooked, place the dish in an oven at low heat or cover the dish and place live coal on top of the lid. 8. Serve garnished with fried onions.

Serves 4.

N.B. Chopped coriander leaves can also be used as a garnish.

3. Moong Dal Khichdi

Pulao rice	500 gm.	Fat	55 gm.
Split green gram	225 gm.	Onions	115 gm.
Cinnamon	a small piece	Turmeric	a pinch
Cloves	6	Salt	10 gm.

1. Wash and soak gram for half an hour. 2. Wash and soak rice for 15 minutes. 3. Heat fat; add sliced onions, spices, salt, turmeric and rice and dal with double the amount of water. 4. Stir and cover the degchi. 5. Cook gently till rice is tender, and khichdi is soft. 6. Garnish with chopped coriander leaves as desired.

Serves 4.

Culinary Cue: If you coat the rim of the vessel with oil or ghee, the khichdi will not boil over.

4. Egg Rice

Pulao rice	*500 gm.*	*Peppercorns*	*10 gm.*
Eggs	*4*	*Cloves*	*6*
Fat	*50 gm.*	*Cinnamon*	*a small piece*
Spring onions	*50 gm.*	*Salt*	*to taste*

1. Wash and boil the rice, adding cinnamon, cloves, salt and peppercorns. 2. Keep the rice warm till you prepare the eggs. 3. Beat the eggs well (white first and then add the yolk); chop onions, with leaves. 4. Heat fat; sauté onions. Add the beaten eggs, cook for a minute or two. 5. Add rice and stir well. Remove and serve hot.

Serves 4.

N.B. Remove cinnamon and cloves before serving the rice.

5. Til Rice

Rice	*500 gm.*	*Salt*	*to taste*
Gingelly seeds	*115 gm.*	*Fat*	*115 gm.*
Red chillies	*5 gm.*	*Curry leaves*	*1 sprig*
Split black gram	*15 gm.*	*Cashewnuts*	*15 gm.*
Asafoetida	*a pinch*	*Lime*	*½*

1. Boil the rice. 2. Heat fat and fry the cashewnuts to a golden brown. Remove and drain. Fry curry leaves. Remove. 3. In the same fat fry cleaned gingelly seeds, red chillies, asafoetida and split black gram. 4. Remove and grind to a powder. 5. Mix the powdered

masala, fried cashewnuts, salt, lime juice and chopped curry leaves with rice.

Serves 4.

6. Vangi Bhath

Rice	500 gm.	Asafoetida	a large pinch
Brinjals (small)	1 kg.	Coriander seeds	5 gm.
Masala		Pepper	a small pinch
Split black gram	115 gm.	Cumin	½ tsp.
Split Bengal gram	115 gm.	Salt	to taste
Chilli powder	2 tsp.	Tamarind	30 gm.
Turmeric	a pinch	Oil	50 ml.
Mustard	2 tsp.		

1. Cook rice. 2. Roast the masala ingredients and powder coarsely. 3. Make a thick extract of tamarind. 4. Wash and cut brinjals into halves. 5. Heat fat. Add brinjals, powdered spices, fry well. Add tamarind extract and salt and simmer till cooked. 6. Add the curry to the rice. Mix well and serve hot.

Serves 4.

7. Vegetable Pulao

Pulao rice	500 gm.	Cardamoms	
Peas	115 gm.	Cinnamon	3 gm.
Beans	115 gm.	Cloves	in all
Carrots	225 gm.	Bay leaf	
Cauliflower	55 gm.	Peppercorns	
Tomatoes	115 gm.	Salt	to taste
Onions	115 gm.	Fat	100 gm.
		Vegetable stock or water	1 litre

1. Shell peas. Peel and cut carrots into long thin slices; string and cut beans also into long slices. Break cauliflower into flowerettes. Slice onions. 2. Wash and drain rice. 3. Heat fat. Fry onions till crisp and remove. 4. Fry vegetables lightly and remove. 5. Add vegetable stock and cook. 7. When rice is three-fourths done make a well in the centre. Add vegetables and chopped tomatoes; cover and cook on a slow fire with live coal on lid or in an oven at low heat. 8. Cook till rice and vegetables are tender. 9. Add salt, mix well and serve hot; garnish with fried onions.

Serves 4.

N.B. The amount of stock or water is approximate. The exact quantity required will depend on the quality of rice and degree of heat.

8. Yakhni Pulao

Yakhni		Pulao	
Mutton	*500 gm.*	*Pulao rice*	*500 gm.*
Onions	*115 gm.*	*Onions*	*115 gm.*
Cinnamon	*a small piece*	*Cumin*	*a pinch*
Cloves	*6*	*Bay leaf*	
Garlic	*a few flakes*	*Cloves*	*3 gm.*
Ginger	*a small piece*	*Cardamom*	*in all*
Green chillies	*5 gm.*	*Cinnamon*	
Garnish		*Curd*	*115 gm.*
Hard boiled egg	*1*	*Salt*	*10 gm.*
		Fat	*50 gm.*

1. Wash and cut up meat. 2. Place all yakhni ingredients in a pan, cover with stock or water and simmer till meat is tender. 3. Allow it to become cold and remove fat from surface. 4. Wash and soak rice. 5. Peel and

slice onions. 6. Heat fat, fry sliced onions and remove. 7. Fry whole spices. 8. Add meat from stock (yakhni) and curd. Cook for 15-20 minutes. 9. Add rice and fry. 10. Add stock and salt and cook till rice is tender. 11. Remove excess moisture by putting live coal on the lid or by drying in an oven. 12. Serve hot, garnished with fried onions and hard boiled egg.
Serves 4.

9. Moghlai Biryani

Pulao rice	400 gm.	Curd	225 gm.
Mutton	500 gm.	Milk	100 ml.
Lime	1	Red chillies	4—5
Almonds or		(without seeds)	
cashewnuts	50 gm.	Turmeric	a pinch
Mint leaves	a few sprigs	Cardamoms	
Fat	115 gm.	Cloves	3 gm. in all
Coriander leaves	¼ bunch	Cinnamon	
Onions	115 gm.	Bay leaf	
Ginger	5 gm.	Sweet cumin	a pinch
Green chillies	5 gm.	Saffron	a little
(chopped fine)		Wheat flour	enough to
Garlic	3 flakes	paste	seal pan

1. Wash, trim and cut the mutton into small pieces. 2. Peel and slice onions; chop coriander leaves and mint. 3. Peel ginger and garlic. 4. Grind ginger, red chillies, garlic, and nuts into a fine paste. 5. Heat fat. Fry onions till golden brown and crisp. Remove. 6. Add bay leaf, ground masala; fry. 7. Add meat; fry. 8. Add tepid water and cook with lid on till meat is tender and gravy is thick. 9. Boil rice till three-fourths cooked. 10. Add salt. 11. Empty curd into a fine piece of muslin and strain. 12. Add to it powdered cloves, cinnamon,

cardamoms, sweet cumin, turmeric, chopped green chillies, coriander leaves and mint. Add lime juice and mix well. 13. Add curd mixture to mutton. Stir well. 14. Dissolve saffron in some milk and sprinkle over half the rice. 15. In a heavy pan arrange layers of rice, mutton and fried onions. Repeat till all ingredients are used up. 16. Pour remaining milk and fat over the rice. Cover pan and seal edges with wheat flour paste. 17. Place in an oven 143°C (300°F) for one hour and serve very hot.
Serves 4.

10. Qorma Biryani

Mutton stock	850 ml.	*Black peppercorns*	8
Mutton	500 gm.	*Bay leaves*	2
Old Basmati rice	400 gm.	*Nutmeg*	½
Ghee	350 gm.	*Javitri*	3—4 pieces
Onions (medium)	2	*Zafrani*	a pinch
Ground ginger	1 ½ tsp.	*Red chilli powder*	¼ tsp.
Green cardamoms	6	*Coriander powder*	2 tsp.
Ground garlic	1 ½ tsp.	*Milk*	2—3 tsp.
Cinnamon	2 one-inch pieces	*Kewra water*	2 tsp.
Cloves	8	*Salt*	to taste

1. Slice onions thinly. In a degchi heat ghee and fry half the onions till they are golden brown and crisp. Remove and spread the onions on paper. 2. Heat some more ghee and fry the green cardamoms, cloves and cinnamon. Cover and let them sizzle for a minute or so. 3 Add the remaining sliced onions. When they turn golden brown add meat, ground ginger and garlic, red chilli powder, coriander powder, salt, and bay leaves and mix well. 4. Add stock in place of water. Cover and let the meat cook on medium fire until it is three-

fourths done, or till the meat and all the ingredients are brown, and ghee and a little liquid are left in the form of curry. While cooking, stir the meat occasionally and keep adding stock or a little water as required. 5. Now soak the rice for about 15 minutes and dissolve the zafrani in kewra water. 6 Grind the fried onions with nutmeg and javitri. 7. In another degchi boil water with peppercorns, a few cloves, one bay leaf and salt and cook rice for about 3-4 minutes, or until it is one-third done, then drain the water out. 8. In a heavy-bottomed pan place the rice and curry in layers starting with the rice at the bottom and covering with rice at the top. 9. Sprinkle the ground nutmeg-onion-javitri mixture, zafrani and a few drops of milk evenly on the top. 10. Place a damp cloth under the lid of the pan and cover it. 11. Place it on a slow fire for about 20 minutes or till you get the aroma.

Serves 4

11. Fried Rice

Rice	*400 gm.*	*Salad oil*	*100 ml.*
Leeks	*200 gm.*	*Tomato ketchup*	*100 ml.*
Carrots	*200 gm.*	*Soyabean sauce*	*40—50 ml.*
Cabbage	*200 gm.*	*Prawns or pork*	*225 gm.*
Onions	*200 gm.*	*Turmeric*	*a pinch*
Celery	*50 gm.*	*Salt*	*to taste*
Eggs	*4*		

1. Cook rice till three-fourths done. 2. Shell prawns. Remove intestines. Wash well, smear turmeric and salt and fry. (If pork is used boil with peppercorns and salt and cut into cubes). 3. Shred vegetables. Heat oil. Add vegetables. Sauté. 4. Add beaten eggs and scramble.

5. Add prawns and rice. Fry for a few minutes. Add sauces. Cover and cook till done. Remove and serve hot with Shanghai Omelette, Capsicum Salad and Chilli Sauce.
Serves 4.

N.B. When fried rice is made in large quantities divide into smaller portions and mix.

SHANGHAI OMELETTE

Eggs	4	Cabbage	15 gm.
Leeks	15 gm.	Onion	15 gm.
Carrots	15 gm.	Capsicum	30 gm.
Flaked crab		Salt	to taste
or prawns	15 gm.	Oil	to shallow fry

1. Wash and shred vegetables. 2. Chop onion and capsicum fine. 3. Beat eggs lightly. Add vegetables, chopped prawns, salt, onion, capsicum and mix. Pour into hot oil and fry lightly like pancakes. Garnish rice with strips of omelette.

CAPSICUM SALAD

Capsicum	115 gm.	Lime	1
Salt	to taste	Sugar	30 gm.

1. Wash capsicum. Remove seeds. 2. Chop and mix with lime juice, sugar and salt.

CHILLI SAUCE

Red capsicum or	225 gm.	Ginger	450 gm.
Red chillies	115 gm.	Sugar	450 gm.
Garlic	450 gm.	Vinegar	710 ml.
		Salt	to taste

1. Remove seeds from capsicum or chillies. 2. Peel and

CEREALS

chop ginger and garlic. 3. Grind together all ingredients, using vinegar. 4. Mix with remaining vinegar.

12. Chapaties

Whole wheat flour	450 gm.	Rice flour	30 gm.
Salt	10 gm.	Fat	20 gm.

1. Sieve wheat flour. 2. Add salt and water and make a stiff dough. 3. Sprinkle some water over and set aside for at least one hour. 4. Knead well. 5. Divide into small balls. 6. Roll out each chapati using rice flour. 7. Bake well on both sides on a hot griddle. 8. Toss on hot coal. Allow it to puff up. 9. Smear with melted fat and serve hot.

Makes 24 chapaties.

N.B. Rice flour used to roll chapaties makes them soft.

13. Stuffed Parathas

Whole wheat flour	115 gm.	Green chillies	5 gm.
Refined flour	115 gm.	Ginger	a small piece
Milk	65 ml.	Garlic	2 flakes
Curd	15 gm.	Salt	to taste
Salt	10 gm.	Garam masala	
Fat	30 gm.	powder	a pinch
Stuffing		Coriander leaves	1 sprig
Boiled potatoes	200 gm.	Onion	30 gm.
Fresh peas	115 gm.	Fat	30 gm.

1. Sieve whole wheat flour and refined flour and rub in fat. Add curd, milk, salt, and water if required, to make a stiff dough. 2. Keep aside for half an hour. 3. Knead well and divide into even portions. 4. Roll into even-

sized rounds. Spread some prepared filling on one. Cover with another. Bind edges with a little milk. 5. Place on a hot greased griddle. 6. Turn when one side is light brown. 7. Add a tsp. of melted fat around. 8. Cook both sides till light brown and crisp.

STUFFING

1. Boil and chop potatoes, shell and crush peas. 2. Heat fat. Add chopped onion, garlic, ginger and green chillies. Add peas or minced meat. Cook on a slow fire. 3. When peas are cooked, add chopped potatoes and remaining ingredients. Stir till dry. Remove and use as required.
Serves 4.

14. Moghlai Parathas

Refined flour	*500 gm.*	*Water to make a soft dough*	
Melted fat		*Fat*	*for frying*
(for dough)	*115 gm.*		
Salt	*to taste*		

1. Sift flour. Add salt. Prepare a soft dough with water. Knead well. Set aside covered for one hour. 2. Divide into 8 portions. Form into balls and set aside for another 15 minutes. 3. Roll each ball into a round 17.5 cm. (7") in diameter. Smear over melted fat. 4. Make a cut from centre to the edge. 5. Roll from one end of the cut side, in the shape of a cone, to the other end. 6. Press cone between palms. Roll out 0.75 cm. (¼") thick rounds. 7. Deep fry till golden brown. Remove and drain. Serve hot.

Makes 8 parathas.

CEREALS

15. Bhaturas

Maida (refined flour)	1 kg.	*Salt*	10—12 gm.
Potatoes	250 gm.	*Fat for frying (absorption)*	150 gm.

1. Peel the potatoes, boil and mash. 2. Sieve the flour, add mashed potatoes, salt and enough water to form a soft dough. 3. Keep aside for half an hour. 4. Roll out puris of 6" diameter. 5. Fry them in hot fat and serve hot.

Serves 15.

Culinary Cue: Traditionally, bhaturas are served with Alu-chhole (for recipe see page 32).

16. Pal Appam (Hoppers)

Rice flour	150 gm.	*Water*	200 ml.
Toddy	100 ml.	*Large size coconut*	½
Coarse rice flour or semolina (sooji)	25 gm.	*Sugar*	30 gm.
		Salt	to taste

1. Roast the rice flour lightly, without addition of fat, in a *karai*. Sieve. 2. To the coarse rice flour, add 200 ml. of water and cook to porridge consistency. 3. Add this and the toddy to the roasted rice flour and knead to a soft dough. Leave overnight to ferment. 4. Grate coconut and prepare 200 to 250 ml. of coconut milk. 5. Add the coconut milk, sugar and salt to the rice flour dough. Cover and let it stand for one hour. 6. Pour a spoonful of butter into a thick iron *karai* (well seasoned). 7. Set for a minute and then take the pan with both hands and give it a circular twist till about one cm. more of the pan all round is thinly coated with the batter

CEREALS 27

which, when the hopper is baked, forms a crisp brown border.

Makes 10 hoppers.

N.B. The inside of the hopper pan should not be washed but greased with a mixture of melted butter and gingelly oil. If the hopper sticks to the pan, fry an egg in the pan, remove, tie in a soft rag and use to grease the pan by dipping it in oil and rubbing it over the bottom of the pan.

17. Methi Ki Roti

Whole wheat flour	100 gm.	*Salt*	5 gm.
Bengal gram flour	50 gm.	*Turmeric*	a pinch
Fenugreek leaves	50 gm.	*Fat*	50 gm.
Coriander leaves	15 gm.		

1. Sieve flour and gram flour together. Add chopped coriander and fenugreek leaves. Add salt, a pinch of turmeric and 15 gm. of fat. 2. Prepare a soft dough using water. Divide into balls and roll each into a thin chapati. Smear with fat. Make into a ball. 3. Roll it again into a chapati. Bake both sides on a hot griddle. 4. Apply fat. Fry for a few minutes and remove.

Serves 6.

18. Spinach Puris

Whole wheat flour	500 gm.	*Salt*	to taste
Spinach purée	120 ml.	*Fat (for the dough)*	30 gm.
Water	50 ml.	*Fat for frying*	

28 CEREALS

1. Sieve flour, spinach purée, water, fat and salt and prepare a mediumly stiff dough. Knead well. Set aside for at least half an hour. 2. Divide the dough into even sized balls. 3. Roll out evenly 10 cm. in diameter approximately. 4. Fry puris in enough oil, gently pressing down with a flat spoon in a circular motion. 5. When puffed up turn over. Lightly brown on both sides. 6. Drain on paper and serve hot.

Makes 50 puris.

DALS

1. Dal

Split red gram	225 gm.	Tempering	
Onion	55 gm.	Fat	10 gm.
Green chillies	10 gm.	Curry leaves	a sprig
Turmeric	a pinch	Mustard seeds	a pinch
Fat	30 gm.	Whole red chillies	3-4
Salt	to taste		

1. Clean and wash gram. 2. Slice onion and slit green chillies. 3. Heat fat. Sauté gram, onion, chillies, turmeric. Add enough water to cook. 4. When tender remove from fire. Mash and add more water if required. 5. Add salt and bring to boil. 6. Remove and temper with given ingredients.

Serves 4.

Culinary Cue: Dals can be preserved longer if you rub a little castor oil on them before storing.

DALS

2. Saag Bhaji

Spinach	*1 bunch*	*Carrot (medium)*	*1*
Chuka (ambadi; roselle leaves)	*1 bunch*	*Potato (medium)*	*1*
		Bottle gourd	*size of a potato*
Suva	*¼ bunch*	*Onion (medium)*	*1*
Fenugreek leaves (leaves only)	*¼ bunch*	*Green chillies*	*2*
		Tomatoes (medium)	*2*
Coriander leaves	*1 ¼ bunch*	*Garlic*	*6 flakes*
Split Bengal gram	*85 gm.*	*Ginger*	*a small piece*
Salt	*to taste*	*Clarified butter*	*1 tbsp.*
Oil	*1 tbsp.*		

1. Slice onion, chop green chillies, garlic and ginger. 2. Wash and cut all the other vegetables. 3. Wash and soak Bengal gram for two to three hours. 4. Heat oil, sauté onion, garlic, ginger and green chillies. 5. Add all the leafy vegetables, carrot, potato and bottle gourd. Place drained gram on top, add chopped tomatoes and salt. 6. Cover pan and cook over slow fire till gram is cooked. 7. Churn well to mash and test for seasoning. 8. Consistency should be thick but not dry. Reheat. Pour clarified butter over and serve.

Serves 15.

N.B. If chuka is not available, add one more tomato.

3. Tur Dal and Vegetable Sorak

Split red gram	*225 gm.*	*Turmeric*	*¼ tsp*
Vegetables (potatoes, bottle gourd, brinjal)		*Onions*	*2*
		Red Chillies	*5*
	225 gm.	*Garlic*	*3 cloves*
Coriander seeds	*2 tbsp.*	*Coconut*	*¼*
Cumin	*½ tsp.*	*Curd*	*1 cup*

Salt	to taste	Curry leaves	2 sprigs
Tempering		Clarified butter	1 tbsp.
Mustard seeds	¼ tsp.		

1. Clean and wash the gram. Wash vegetables and cut them even-sized. Boil gram and vegetables. 2. Grind spices, onions and grated coconut to a fine paste. Mix in beaten curd. Add to the gram. 3. Stir well and bring to a boil. Add salt. Remove. 4. Heat clarified butter in a frying pan. Add curry leaves and mustard seeds. As seeds splutter, pour over prepared dish. Stir well. 5. Serve hot.

Serves 6.

4. Rasam

Split red gram	30 gm.	Peppercorns	a few
Tamarind	10 gm.	Cumin seeds	a pinch
Coriander leaves	¼ bunch	Garlic	1 flake
Salt	15 gm.	Tempering	
Masala		Oil	15 ml.
Red chillies	2—3	Red chilli	1
Asafoetida	a pinch	Mustard seeds	1 tsp.
Coriander seeds	5 gm.	Curry leaves	1 sprig

1. Cook gram in about two litres of water till tender. 2. Squeeze tamarind in a little water. 3. Roast and pound spices. 4. Mix together the liquid in which the gram was cooked, the mashed up gram, pounded masala, tamarind juice and salt to taste. 5. Bring to boil. 6. Remove and temper with mustard seeds, whole red chilli and curry leaves.

Serves 6.

5. Garlic Kadhi

Coconut	½	Garlic	4 gm.
Red chillies	2	Cocum	5 gm.
(Sankeshwari)		Salt	to taste
Peppercorns	1 gm.	Coriander leaves	2 sprigs

1. Grind together coconut, red chillies, peppercorns, garlic and cocum. 2. And one cup of water. Keep aside for about ten minutes and extract juice. 3. Add salt and chopped coriander leaves.

Serves 4.

Culinary Cue: This kadhi goes very well with rice and Goan fried fish (see page 54). Ask anyone from the west coast!

6. Alu Chhole

Bengal gram	225 gm.	Chilli powder	½ tsp.
Soda bicarb	1 tsp.	Green chillies	3
Large cardamom	1	Tamarind	30 gm.
Cinnamon powder	½ tsp.	Onion	55 gm.
Cumin powder	½ tsp.	Tomatoes	55 gm.
Pepper powder	½ tsp.	Potatoes	115 gm.
Clove powder	½ tsp.	Salt	to taste
Coriander powder	½ tsp.	Coriander leaves	2 sprigs
Turmeric	⅛ tsp.	Fat	15 gm.

1. Wash and soak gram overnight with soda bicarb. 2. Cook gram till tender. 3. Add powdered cardamom, cinnamon, cumin, clove, pepper and coriander and cook. 4. Heat half the fat. Fry sliced onion, turmeric and chilli powder. 5. Add gram, tomatoes and whole green chillies. 6. Continue cooking and mash gram. 7. Just before removing from the fire add tamarind

juice and salt. 8. Boil potatoes and slice. 9. Fry half of the sliced potatoes and add to the gram. 10. Serve garnished with boiled and sliced potatoes and chopped coriander leaves.

Serves 4.

N.B. Serve with hot puris or bhaturas.

7. Makhani Dal

Black gram (whole)	*250 gm.*	*Red chilli powder*	*5 gm.*
Kidney beans	*50 gm.*	*Turmeric*	*¼ tsp.*
Onion	*1*	*Oil*	*30 ml.*
Tomato	*1 large*	*Ghee (clarified butter)*	*60 gm.*
Ginger	*2" piece*	*Cumin seeds*	*½ tsp.*
Garlic	*½ pod*	*Salt*	*to taste*
Green chillies	*10 gm.*	*Coriander leaves*	*2 sprigs*

1. Clean and soak gram and beans separately for at least four hours. 2. Boil kidney beans. When half cooked, add gram and oil and boil till both are well cooked. Add salt. 3. Heat half the ghee. Add cumin seeds, sliced ginger, sliced onion, green chillies and chopped garlic; fry till golden brown. 4. Add turmeric, chilli powder and chopped tomatoes and fry till tomatoes are cooked. 5. Add gram and beans and half of the chopped coriander leaves. 6. Cook on a slow fire, stirring constantly, for another 20 minutes. 7. Add the remaining ghee and remove from fire. 8. Garnish with remaining chopped coriander leaves.

Serves 4.

Culinary Cue: If you forget to soak the gram or beans, cook for a few minutes in boiling water. After an hour, they are ready for use.

VEGETABLES

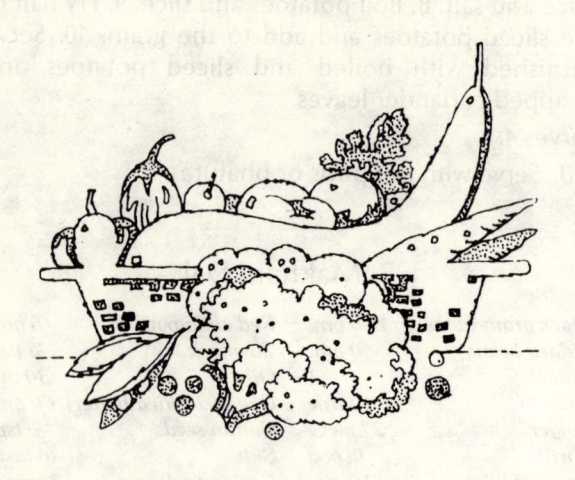

1. Onion Cuchumber

Onions	*225 gm.*	*Lime*	*15 gm.*
Coriander leaves	*¼ bunch*	*Salt*	*to taste*
Green chillies	*5 gm.*		

1. Slice the onions into medium sized strips. 2. Chop coriander leaves and green chillies and mix with onions, lime juice and salt.

Serves 4.

N.B. Add finely chopped tomatoes to onion cuchumber to prepare tomato cuchumber.

2. Cabbage Salad

Cabbage (fresh)	*225 gm.*	*Salad oil*	*30 ml.*
Onion	*55 gm.*	*Lime*	*1*

Green chillies	5	*Salt*	*to taste*
Coriander leaves	*½ bunch*		

1. Shred cabbage fine. Chop green chillies, onion and coriander leaves. Extract juice from lime. 2. Mix all ingredients together.

Serves 4.

Culinary Cue: For extra crispness, dip the cabbage in iced water before shredding.

3. Fried Lady's Fingers

Lady's fingers (okra)	10	*Red onions*	2
Red chillies	5	*Turmeric*	*¼ tsp.*
Peppercorns	10	*Salt*	*to taste*
Garlic	*1 flake*	*Oil*	*2 dsp.*

1. Wipe lady's fingers with a wet cloth. 2. Cut into one-inch lengths. 2. Grind together all spices. 4. Heat one dsp. oil. Fry lady's fingers. 5. Add ground spices and salt. Mix well. 6. Add just enough water to cook dry. Remove and fry in remaining oil.

Serves 4

N.B. Wiping the lady's fingers prevents stickiness.

4. Beans Foogath

French beans	*450 gm.*	*Oil*	*30 ml.*
Onion	*55 gm.*	*Coconut*	*55 gm.*
Green chillies	*5 gm.*	*Salt*	*to taste*
Mustard seeds	*a pinch*	*Curry leaves*	*1 sprig*

1. Wash, string and slice beans into fine round pieces. 2. Chop onion and green chillies. 3. Heat oil. Add

mustard seeds. 4. When mustard seeds crackle, add chopped onions, green chillies and curry leaves. Sauté. 5. Add sliced beans, salt and enough water to cook beans. 6. Cook till beans are done and all water has evaporated. 7. Add grated coconut, cook a little longer, stir well and remove from fire. Serve hot.

Serves 4.

5. Cauliflower Bhujia

Cauliflower	450 gm.	Mustard seeds or	½ tsp.
Onion	55 gm.	cumin seeds	
Dry mango powder	½ tsp.	Turmeric	½ tsp.
Ginger	a small piece	Garlic	3 flakes
Green chillies	2	Fat	15 gm.
Salt	to taste		

1. Break cauliflower into small flowerettes and wash. 2. Slice onion and half the garlic, ginger and chillies. Grind the remainder. 3. Heat fat. Add mustard seeds or cumin seeds. When seeds crackle, add turmeric and sliced ingredients and fry well. Add ground spices and cauliflower. Add salt. 4. Cook over gentle heat with lid on till cauliflower is cooked. 5. Add mango powder. Stir well and remove.

Serves 4.

N.B. Tomatoes may be substituted for mango powder, in which case, cook for a further five to ten minutes after adding tomatoes.

6. Tomato Mahasha

Tomatoes (even-sized,		Potatoes	225 gm.
medium ripe)	500 gm.	Fat	50 gm.

VEGETABLES 37

Lentils	*225 gm.*	*Salt*	*to taste*
Onions	*100 gm.*	*Refined wheat*	
Green chillies	*2*	*flour for paste*	*15 gm.*

1. Cut tops off tomatoes and scoop out pulp. Sprinkle with salt and place inverted on racks. 2. Boil and mash lentils and potatoes. 3. Chop onions and chillies. 4. Heat part of the fat and fry onions. 5. Mix together onions, chillies and salt with mashed lentils and potatoes. 6. Cool mixture and fill tomatoes. 7. Firmly press down stuffing. Put tops of tomatoes on, like lids, and seal with flour-and-water paste. 8. Heat fat. Fry the tomatoes first on sealed side. When browned, turn and fry all over. Cook covered till tomatoes are quite soft.

Serves 4.

Culinary Cue: To prevent the tomatoes from breaking, dip them in a little vinegar before frying.

7. Shuktoni

Chowli beans	*10 gm.*	*Milk*	*20 ml.*
Brinjals	*2*	*Salt*	*5—7 gm. to taste*
Potatoes	*150 gm. (2)*	*Sugar*	*2 gm.*
Drumsticks	*30 gm.*	*Fat*	*30 gm.*
Broad beans	*100 gm.*	*Dry mixed spices*	
Radish	*2 gm. (1 slice)*	*Fenugreek seeds*	*a pinch*
Peas	*100 gm.*	*Onion seeds*	*a pinch*
Bitter gourd	*50 gm. (2)*	*Fennel*	*a pinch*
Ginger	*5 gm. (2.5 cm. piece)*	*Cumin*	*a pinch*
Turmeric powder	*1 gm. (¼ tsp.)*	*Mustard seeds*	*a pinch*
Mustard seeds	*2 gm.*		

1. Cut beans, brinjals, peeled potatoes, radish and

bitter gourd into long pieces and fry separately. 2. Cut drumsticks into long pieces and shell peas. 3. Grind ginger, mustard seeds and turmeric to a smooth paste. 4. Heat fat, fry dry mixed spices and curry leaves. Add vegetables and fry a little. 5. Add ground spices, salt, sugar and enough water to cook the vegetables. Cover and simmer till vegetables are tender. 6. Add milk and cook till the gravy becomes thick.

Serves 8.

8. Palak Panir

Spinach	455 gm.	Green chillies	5 gm.
Cottage cheese		Chilli powder	5 gm.
(panir)	115 gm.	Coriander leaves	a few
Ginger	a small piece	Fat	30 gm.
Garlic	a few flakes	Salt	to taste

1. Cut panir into cubes. 2. Heat fat. Fry panir till light brown, and remove. 3. Grind together chilli powder, garlic and ginger. 4. Fry spices and whole green chillies. 5. Add washed and chopped spinach. Sauté. 6. Add salt. Cook for a few minutes. Add water if necessary. Cover and cook on slow fire till spinach is cooked. Mash well. 7. Add panir cubes. Bring to boil and remove. Garnish with chopped coriander leaves.

Serves 4.

9. Panir Makhani

Panir (cut into	400 gm.	Bay leaves	2 gm.
2.5 cm. 1" thick slices)		Peppercorns	2 gm.
Tomato purée (fresh)	250 gm.	Garam masala powder	5 gm.
Onion	50 gm.	Kasoori methi powder	5 gm.

VEGETABLES 39

Ginger-garlic paste	25 gm.	Cloves	2 gm.
Red chilli paste	20 gm.	Cream	50 ml.
Cinnamon	2 gm.	Butter	50 gm.
Cardamoms	2 gm.	Oil	50 gm.

1. Fry panir slices till golden brown and soak in water. 2. Heat oil in a pan. Add whole garam masala, chopped onion and brown. 3. Add ginger-garlic paste and cook. Add red chilli paste, tomato purée, garam masala powder, kasoori methi powder and cook for a few minutes. 4. Add panir and finally cream and butter. Garnish the dish with juliennes of ginger and green chillies and cream.

Serves 4.

10. Cashew Potato Curry

Potatoes	125 gm. (2 medium)	Onions	2 (200 gm.)
Cashewnuts (preferably green tender ones)	75 gm.	Green chillies	2 (2 gm.)
		Ginger	10 gm.
		Garlic	4 cloves (2 gm.)
Red chillies	2 (2 gm.)	Coconut	½
Turmeric	¼ tsp. (1 gm.)	Oil	2 tbsp. (25 ml.)
Coriander seeds	1 tbsp. (8 gm.)	Curry leaves	a sprig
		Mustard seeds	a pinch
Cumin	a pinch (1 gm.)	Salt	to taste
Lime	½		

1. Peel and cut potatoes into 5 cm. (2") pieces. Soak cashewnuts in hot water. 2. Grate coconut. Extract coconut milk from three-fourths of the coconut (twice). 3. Boil cashewnuts and potatoes in the second extract of coconut milk. 4. Grind to a fine paste the remaining coconut, red chillies, coriander seeds, turmeric and cumin. 5. Slice onions and slit green

chillies. Slice ginger and garlic. 6. Heat the oil. Add mustard seeds and curry leaves. When seeds splutter add ground spices and sliced ingredients. Cook till onions are soft. 7. Add cooked vegetables, lime juice and salt. Simmer for 10 minutes. 8. Add the first extract of coconut milk and simmer for 5 minutes. Test for seasoning and remove.

Serves 4.

N.B. Instead of potatoes, mushrooms or drumsticks may be used.

11. Pavakkai Varatharacha Curry
(Bitter Gourd Curry)

Bitter gourd	2 big gourds	*Medium-sized coconut*	1
Green chillies	4	*Red onion(b)*	1
Salt	to taste	*Garlic(b)*	1 flake
Red chillies	10	*Curry leaves*	a few sprigs
Coriander seeds	2 tbsp.	Tempering	
Turmeric	1.25 cm. (½" piece)	*Oil*	2 tbsp.
		Mustard seeds	½ tsp.
Red onion(a)	1	*Onion (small)*	1
Garlic(a)	2 flakes		
Tamarind ball the size of 1 lime	(3.5 cm. diameter)		

1. Wash and dry gourd. Cut lengthwise. Remove seeds and cut into pieces 0.75 cm. by 3.75 cm. (¼"×1 ½"). 2. Parboil with salt and slit green chillies, till cooked dry. 3. Roast well and grind together red chillies, coriander seeds, turmeric, red onion(a) and garlic(a). 4. Soak tamarind in one cup water. 5. Mix the ground ingredients above with tamarind pulp and add to

bitter gourd. Add more salt if desired. Simmer till thick gravy remains. 6. Grate coconut fine and roast with red onion(b), garlic(b) and curry leaves till well browned. Grind to a fine paste. 7. Mix with one cup of water and add to bitter gourd. Taste to ensure that the dish has enough salt and sourness. 8. Bring to boil. 9. Heat oil; add mustard seeds. 10. When seeds crackle, add small onion (sliced), and brown. 11. Add prepared bitter gourd and remove.

Serves 8.

Variations: Elephant yam, snake gourd, brinjal, etc. can be used instead of bitter gourd.

12. Alu Bhurta

Potatoes	220 gm.	*Mustard seeds*	½ tsp.
Onion	50 gm.	*Chilli powder*	1 tsp.
Green chillies	5 gm.	*Salt*	10 gm.
Lime	1	*Coriander*	
Fat	30 gm.	*leaves*	*a few sprigs*

1. Boil potatoes. Peel and mash. 2. Chop green chillies and onion. 3. Heat fat. Add mustard seeds. When they crackle remove pan from fire and add chilli powder. 4. Add chopped onion, green chillies, mashed potatoes, salt and lime juice. Mix well. 5. Serve garnished with coriander leaves.

Serves 4.

13. Til Alu Dum

Potatoes (boiled, peeled		*Til (roasted and*	
and cubed)	250 gm.	*powdered)*	60 gm.

VEGETABLES

Salt	*to taste*	*Asafoetida*	*1 tsp.*
Tempering		*Timur (optional)*	*¼ tsp.*
Oil	*50 ml.*	*Lime*	*½*
Fenugreek seeds	*2 gm.*	*Turmeric*	*¼ tsp.*
Green chillies	*10 gm.*		

1. Mix together cubed potatoes, roasted and powdered til seeds and salt. 2. Heat oil, add fenugreek seeds. As they splutter add green chillies, turmeric, asafoetida and, if you like timur. 4. Pour over potato mixture. Add lime juice and mix well.

Serves 4.

14. Doodhi Kofta Curry

Bottle gourd	*225 gm.*	Gravy	
Onion	*30 gm.*	*Tomatoes*	*200 gm.*
Bengal gram flour	*30 gm.*	*Onions*	*100 gm.*
Green chillies	*2—3*	*Red chilli powder*	*5 gm.*
Ginger	*5 gm.*	*Turmeric*	*a pinch*
Coriander leaves	*¼ bunch*	*Coriander powder*	*10 gm.*
Oil to fry koftas		*Cumin*	*a pinch*
and for gravy	*50 ml.*	*Garam masala*	*a pinch*
		Salt	*to taste*

1. Peel and grate bottle gourd. Remove excess moisture by squeezing (Keep aside the liquid). 2. Chop fine the green chillies, ginger, coriander leaves and onions. 3. Mix with grated gourd, gram flour and salt. Form into even-sized balls. 4. Heat oil. Deep fry koftas and set aside.

TO PREPARE GRAVY

1. Grind spices to a fine paste. Slice onions. Chop tomatoes. 2. Heat oil. Add sliced onions and fry well.

Add chopped tomatoes, grated spices, salt, liquid from the grated gourd, and water (about 300 ml. or one glass). Bring to boil. 3. Simmer till gravy is thick. Add fried koftas. 4. Bring to boil. Check for seasoning and remove. Serve hot.

Makes 8 koftas.

15. Vegetable Kababs

Potatoes	100 gm.	*Cloves*	1 gm.
Carrots	100 gm.	*Cinnamon*	1 gm.
Beans	100 gm.	*Green chillies*	10 gm.
Cauliflower	100 gm.	*Egg*	1
Onions	100 gm.	*Lime*	¼
Split Bengal gram	50 gm.	*Oil (absorption)*	65 gm.
Coriander leaves	¼ bunch	*Salt*	10 gm.
Cumin powder	1 gm.		

1. Boil gram. 2. Peel potatoes and boil. 3. Chop fine carrots, cauliflower and beans. 4. Chop onions and green chillies fine too. 5. Heat one tbsp. oil. Add onions and green chillies. Sauté. Add finely chopped vegetables. 6. Stir constantly till cooked. 7. Add mashed gram (dal) and potatoes. 8. Add powdered cumin, cloves and cinnamon. Mix well on the fire. Remove. 9. Add salt and chopped coriander leaves and egg. Mix well. 10. Add lime juice. 11. Shape into balls, flatten and shallow fry till light brown.

Makes 16 kababs.

16. Stuffed Capsicum

Capsicums (large)	450 gm.	*Turmeric*	a pinch
Potatoes	450 gm.	*Fat*	30 gm.

44 VEGETABLES

Green chillies	4—5	Mustard seeds	a few
Cheese	30 gm.	Lime	½
Coriander leaves	¼ bunch	Salt	to taste

1. Slice the tops of capsicums. 2. Remove seeds, wash, apply salt on the inside and keep upside down on a rack. 3. Boil and chop potatoes; temper with mustard seeds. Add chopped green chillies, coriander leaves, turmeric and salt to taste. 4. Mix well, add lime juice. 5. Stuff capsicums with prepared stuffing. Top with cheese. 6. Heat fat in a frying pan and cook capsicums on a very slow fire till soft. 7. Serve hot.

Serves 4.

17. Sikandari Gobhi

Cauliflowers (medium size)	4	Black salt	5 gm.
Curd	300 ml.	Salt	to taste
Garam masala	10 gm.	Cream	50 ml.
Kasoori methi powder	6 gm.	Butter	20 gm.
White pepper powder	5 gm.	Lemons	3

1. Clean the cauliflower and cut into big flowerettes. 2. Mix all the other ingredients together except cream and butter. 3. Marinate the cauliflower in the above mixture for at least one to one and a half hours. 4. Thread the flowerettes into a skewer and grill over charcoal. 5. Mix with cream and butter in a pan to make a thick gravy. 6. Serve garnished with chopped coriander leaves and onion rings.

Serves 4.

18. Doodhi Pachadi

Bottle gourd	450 gm.	Ginger	5 gm.
Onions	115 gm.	Green chillies	5 gm.

Curd	225 gm.	Curry leaves	1 spring
Salt	10 gm.	Onion	5 gm.
Tempering		Red chilli	1
Mustard seeds	a pinch	Oil 15 ml.	

1. Wash, peel and dice the gourd. 2. Chop ginger, slit green chillies and slice onions. 3. Cook all the above ingredients with just enough water to cook the vegetable. 4. Remove from fire, add beaten curd and salt. Heat oil. Add mustard seeds, curry leaves, sliced onions and whole red chilli. When seeds crackle, pour over gourd and curd mixture. Mix well.

Serves 4.

19. Onion Raita

Curd	225 gm.	Coriander leaves	¼ bunch
Onions	115 gm.	Cumin (optional)	a pinch
Green chillies	5 gm.	Salt	to taste

1. Peel and slice onions. Chop green chillies and coriander leaves. 2. Roast and powder cumin if used. 3. Beat curd and mix all ingredients together.

Serves 4.

Culinary Cue: An excellent accompaniment for all kinds of pulaos and biryanis.

20. Mango/Green Tomato Pachhadi

Mangoes, matured but not ripe	1	Coconut	1
		Mustard seeds	¼ tsp.
or		Curry leaves	1 sprig
Green tomatoes	250 gm.		

Small onions	*100 gm.*	*Oil*	*15 ml.*
Shankeshwari chillies	*10 gm.*	*Salt*	*to taste*

1. Peel mangoes before use. Slice and crush. (Remove excess liquid if mangoes are sour). If tomatoes are used, cut them lengthwise into quarter inch pieces.
2. Peel and crush onions and chillies on a stone.
3. Grate coconut and extract milk, the first one thick and the second one thinner. Total liquid should be about 500 ml. 4. Mix all the ingredients together and heat gently. Remove from fire. 5. Heat oil. Add mustard seeds and curry leaves. When the seeds crackle, pour over the pachhadi.
Serves 3-4.

N.B. If tomatoes are used, cook in the third extract of coconut milk with salt for a few minutes.

21. Moru Kulambu

Buttermilk	*½ litre*	*Any vegetable (pumpkin,*	
Coconut	*½*	*green leaves, or*	
Turmeric	*1 tsp.*	*potatoes, or fried*	
Green chillies	*6—7*	*lady's fingers)*	*250 gm.*
Ginger	*2.5 cm. (1") piece*	*Oil*	*1 tbsp.*
Cumin	*2 tsp.*	*Asafoetida*	*a pinch*
Bengal gram flour	*1 tbsp.*	*Curry leaves*	*1 sprig*
Salt	*to taste*	*Mustard seeds*	*a pinch*
		Split black gram	*1 tsp.*

1. Grate coconut and grind to a fine paste with green chillies, cumin and ginger. 2. Mix all the ingredients, down to gram flour, with buttermilk. 3. Add salt and cut vegetables. Heat, stirring, and as the mixture comes to a boil, remove. 4. Heat oil. Add black gram and, as it

browns, add mustard seeds. When seeds crackle, add asafoetida and curry leaves. 5. Pour over the vegetable and curd mixture. Stir well.

Serves 20.

22. Ginger Curry

Ginger	30 gm.	Red chillies	15 gm.
Green chillies	2	Fenugreek seeds	2—3 gm.
Coconut	30 gm.	Tamarind	10—15 gm.
Salt	to taste	Molasses or sugar	5 gm.
Coconut oil	20 ml.	Curry leaves	a few
Mustard seeds	a pinch		

1. Peel and chop the ginger fine and soak in a little hot water. 2. Chop the green chillies. 3. Slice and chop coconut into small pieces. 4. Drain ginger. Place ginger, chillies, curry leaves, coconut in a pan. Add a little water and salt. Cook over a slow fire till dry. 5. Roast red chillies and fenugreek seeds and powder fine. 6. Soak tamarind in a little hot water. 7. Heat oil in a pan. Add mustard seeds. When they crackle add cooked ginger, etc. Sauté. 8. As the mixture turns reddish brown, remove from fire. 9. Add red chilli and fenugreek powder. Add tamarind water. Return to fire. Add salt. 10. Add molasses and bring to boil. Simmer for a few minutes. Remove from fire.

Serves 4.

23. Brinjal Patiala

Brinjal (round variety)	450 gm.	Fennel (saunf)	½ tbsp.
		Sultanas	20 gm.

Fat	to fry	*Cashewnuts*	*20 gm.*
Tomato (small)	*1 (55 gm.)*	*Turmeric*	*5 gm.*
Green chillies	*5 gm. (3—4)*	*Red chillies*	*10 gm.*
Ginger	*10 gm.*	*Onion*	*55 gm.*
Garlic	*5 gm.*	*Salt*	to taste
Fenugreek	*¼ tsp.*	*Coriander leaves*	*¼ bunch*
Kalonjee			
(onion seeds)	*½ tbsp.*		

1. Wash and cut brinjals into long slices. Slice onions. Grind garlic. Cut ginger into juliennes. Slit green chillies. Cut red chillies into thin long strips. Remove seeds. 2. Heat fat. Fry brinjals till tender. Remove. 3. In the same fat fry onions till golden. Add kalonjee, fenugreek, fennel, garlic paste and ginger juliennes. Add sultanas and cashewnuts, red and green chillies, salt and turmeric. Fry for 2 minutes. 4. Add fried brinjal. Mix and cook on slow fire with the lid on for 10 minutes. 5. Place slices of tomatoes on top and cook covered for another 5 minutes. 6. Serve garnished with chopped coriander leaves.

Serves 4.

24. Bhagare Baingan

Brinjals (small size)	*500 gm.*	*Green chillies*	*10 gm.*
Mustard seeds	*2 gm.*	*Cashewnut paste*	*30 gm.*
Methi seeds	*2 gm.*	*Peanut butter*	*5 gm.*
Til seeds	*2 gm.*	*Salt*	*10 gm.*
Kalonji seeds	*2 gm.*	*White pepper powder*	*10 gm.*
Cumin	*2 gm.*	*Curd*	*50 gm.*
Oil	*50 gm.*	*Cream*	*25 ml.*
Onion (chopped)	*50 gm.*	*Aniseed*	*2 gm.*

1. Wash and slit the brinjals into quarters and deep fry

VEGETABLES 49

till brown in colour. 2. Heat oil, add mustard seeds, methi seeds, til seeds, cumin, aniseed, kalonji seeds, chopped onions and green chillies and sauté well. 3. Add curd and brinjals and cook till brinjals are tender. 4. Round off by adding peanut butter, cashewnut paste and cream. 5. Serve hot garnished with chopped coriander leaves.

Serves 4.

EGGS

1. Egg & Potato Curry

Eggs	4	Coconut	½
Potatoes	225 gm.	Green chillies	2
Onions	115 gm.	Ginger	2 gm.
Red chillies	5 gm.	Curry leaves	1 sprig
Coriander seeds	10 gm.	Salt	5 gm.
Turmeric	1 gm.	Vinegar	10 ml.
Cinnamon } Cloves }	½ gm.	Oil	30 ml.

1. Hard boil eggs. Crack and cool in water. Shell and keep aside. 2. Peel potatoes. Quarter and steep in cold water. 3. Slice onions. Chop ginger, grate coconut. 4. Roast red chillies, coriander seeds and turmeric and grind to a fine paste. 5. Grind coconut also to a smooth paste. 6. Heat half of the oil. Sauté sliced onions leaving aside a few slices for tempering. 7. Add ginger,

whole green chillies and ground spices. When well fried, add ground coconut and fry for two minutes. 8. Add potatoes, water and salt and cook till potatoes are tender. 9. Add eggs, cut into halves, and vinegar. Remove from fire. 10. Heat remaining oil in a pan. Brown onions, crushed cloves and cinnamon. Add curry leaves and pour over curry.

Serves 4.

2. Egg and Vegetable Moilee

Eggs	4	*Ginger*	*10 gm.*
Potatoes	*250 gm.*	*Turmeric*	*2—3 gm.*
Cauliflower	*100 gm.*	*Coconut*	*1*
Carrots	*100 gm.*	*Salt*	*5—10 gm.*
Tomatoes	*150 gm.*	*Lime*	*½—1*
Onions	*200 gm.*	*Oil*	*15 ml.*
Green chillies	*6 gm. (2)*		

1. Hardboil the eggs. Crack and put into water. 2. Peel potatoes and quarter. Wash cauliflower and break into flowerettes with the leaves. 3. Peel carrots and cut into 2.5 cm. (1") pieces. 4. Peel and slice onions and ginger. Slit green chillies. 5. Grate coconut and prepare three extracts, thick, medium and thin. Extract lime juice. 6. Heat oil, sauté onions, green chillies and ginger and cook till the onion slices are tender. 7. Add turmeric and potatoes. Sauté for a few minutes. 8. Add third extract of coconut milk and cook gently till potatoes are three-fourths done. 9. Add carrots, cauliflower and salt. Simmer for a further 5 to 10 minutes. 10. Add chopped tomatoes and second extract of coconut milk. Simmer. 11. Add lime juice and test for seasoning.

52 EGGS

12. Now add shelled eggs cut into halves. Bring to boil.
13. Add first extract of coconut milk. Turn off the fire and mix gently.

Serves 4.

N.B. Peas may be added, if desired.

FISH

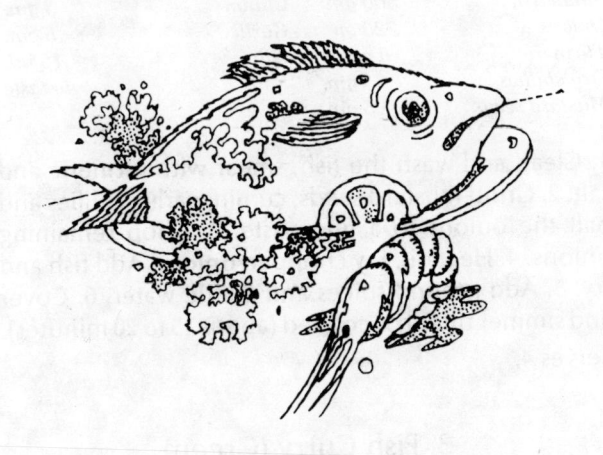

1. Fish Fry (Punjabi)

Fish (fresh-water)	500 gm.	Chilli powder	1 tsp.
Onions	100 gm.	Salt	1 tsp.
Ginger	5 gm.	Dry mango powder	1 tsp.
Cumin	1 tsp.	Garam masala	½ tsp.
Garlic	3-4 flakes	Fat to fry	30 gm.
Turmeric	½ tsp.	(absorption)	

1. Scale and clean fish. Skin and remove bones. Wash well. 2. Cut into 7.5 cm. × 3.5 cm. (approx. 3" × 1½") pieces. 3. Grind spices (onions to garam masala) and smear over the fish. 4. Set aside for about three hours. 5. Deep fry lightly. Remove and drain. 6. When about to serve deep fry again.

Serves 4.

N.B. Serve with tamarind or mint chutney.

2. Fish Fry (Goan)

Small fish	*500 gm.*	*Cumin*	*3 gm.*
Onions	*225 gm.*	*Garlic*	*5 gm.*
Turmeric	*a pinch*	*Oil*	*15 ml.*
Dry chillies	*5 gm.*	*Salt*	*to taste*
Mustard seeds	*5 gm.*		

1. Clean and wash the fish, smear with turmeric and salt. 2. Grind mustard seeds, cumin, garlic, chillies and half the onions to a fine paste. 3. Chop remaining onions. 4. Heat oil. Fry chopped onions. Add fish and fry. 5. Add ground spices and a little water. 6. Cover and simmer till fish is cooked (about 15 to 20 minutes).

Serves 4.

3. Fish Curry (Green)

Fish	*450 gm.*	*Coconut*	*30 gm.*
Ginger	*½ inch*	*Cumin*	*¼ tsp.*
Garlic	*8—9 cloves*	*Fennel*	*¼ tsp.*
Turmeric	*¼ tsp.*	*Green Chillies*	*4—5*
Coriander leaves	*1 bunch*	*Lemon*	*½*
Salt	*to taste*	*Oil*	*30 ml.*

1. Wash, clean and cut fish. Wash again. Apply salt. 2. Grind coconut, cumin, fennel, ginger, turmeric, green chillies and three-fourths of the garlic. When almost ground, add coriander. 3. Add juice of half a lemon. 4. Heat oil and fry two to three cloves of bruised garlic; add spices and water and a little salt. Cook till required amount of gravy remains. 5. Add fish, simmer till fish is cooked. 6. Serve with lemon.

Serves 4.

N.B. If green mangoes are in season, no lemon is required. Skin mangoes, slice, place in curry at the same time as fish.

4. Fish Moilee

Pomfret, salmon, jew		Coconut	1
fish mullet, etc.	500 gm.	Curry leaves	1 sprig
Onion	55 gm.	Oil	15 ml.
Ginger	10 gm.	Garlic	a few flakes
Salt	to taste	Green chillies	10 gm.
Vinegar	10 ml.	Potatoes	225 gm.
Lime	1 (large)	Turmeric	a large pinch
Water	115 ml.		

1. Clean fish, wash in several rinses of cold water and cut it. 2. Peel and slice garlic, ginger, and onion; slit green chillies into two. Peel and cut potatoes. Make two extracts of coconut milk. 3. Heat oil, sauté sliced onion. Add turmeric and cook for two or three minutes. 4. Add garlic, ginger, curry leaves, green chillies, fish and potatoes. 5. Add second extract of coconut milk and salt and cook gently. 6. When cooked add the thick first extract of coconut milk. 7. Bring to boiling point. 8. Add lime juice and vinegar. Serve hot.

Serves 4.

5. Machi Koliwada

Bekti fish (fillet)	500 gm.	Salt	to taste
Bengal gram flour	50 gm.	Ajwain (oregano)	a pinch
Red chilli powder	10 gm.	Eggs	2
Ginger-garlic paste	10 gm.	Lemon juice or vinegar	1 tsp.
		Oil	to fry

1. Clean fish and fillet. Wash well in several rinses of cold water. Marinade in lime juice and salt or vinegar and salt. 2. Beat eggs. 3. Make a batter with gramflour and ginger-garlic paste. Add salt, ajwain and red chilli powder. 4. Dip fish in the batter and deep fry till crisp on the outside and moist and tender inside.
Serves 4.

6. Patrani Machhi

Pomfret	455 gm.	Salt	10 gm.
Fresh coconut	½ (115) gm.	Sugar	a pinch
Green chillies	5 gm.	Garlic	a few flakes
Coriander leaves	1 bunch	Vinegar	115 ml.
Cumin	1 tsp.	Fat	50 gm.
Lime	1		

1. Clean and slice fish, wash well. 2. Grind together coconut, green chillies, garlic, cumin, coriander leaves, salt and sugar. And lime juice. 3. Wipe fish slices with a dry cloth and coat with ground ingredients. 4. Wrap in banana leaves. 5. Heat together vinegar and fat. 6. Immerse fish in the heated vinegar and fat. 7. Cover with a lid and put live coal on top or place in warm oven. 8. Cook gently till fish is tender.
Serves 4.

7. Fish In Sauce (Parsi style)

Pomfret	500 gm.	Onions	225 gm.
Cherry tomatoes	55 gm.	Cumin	½ tsp.
Chilli powder	1 tsp.	Coriander leaves	¼ bunch
Garlic	½ pod	Green chillies	5 gm.
Salt	to taste	Eggs	2
Sugar	½ tsp.	Vinegar	50 ml.
Refined flour	30 gm.	Cinnamon	1.75 cm. (½")
Fat	50 gm.		

1. Clean, wash and cut pomfret into slices. Apply salt and set aside. 2. Chop onions, coriander leaves and green chillies fine. 3. Grind cumin, cinnamon and garlic. 4. Wash tomatoes. 5. Heat fat, sauté onions. Add ground spices and fry. Add chilli powder and chopped ingredients. 6. Add flour, stir well. Add hot water to form a thick sauce. Cover with lid and bring to boil. 7. When it starts boiling add fish. 8. When fish is cooked add whole tomatoes and remove. 9. When sauce cools add eggs beaten with vinegar and sugar. 10. Reheat but do not boil, to prevent curdling. Serve hot.

Serves 4.

8. Machlisalan (Punjabi)

Cod or halibut or jew fish	500 gm.	*Garlic*	2 flakes
Chilli powder	1 tsp.	*Onions*	225 gm.
Coriander powder	5 gm.	*Tomatoes*	500 gm.
Turmeric	½ tsp.	*Salt*	to taste
Garam masala	1 tsp.	*Fat*	30 gm.

1. Clean and cut fish into large pieces. 2. Grind together chilli powder, coriander powder, turmeric, garam masala and salt. 3. Smear well on fish and set aside for an hour. 4. Slice onions and garlic. Chop tomatoes. 5. Heat fat. Fry onions till light brown. 6. Add fish and tomatoes and a little water if necessary. 7. Bring to boil and simmer for about 20 minutes over a gentle fire.

Serves 4.

Culinary Cue: To store fish in the refrigerator, put it into a pan of water to retain its delicate flavour.

9. Malayalee Fish Curry (Meen Vevichathu)

Large fish like pomfret, mullet, bekti, hilsa, salmon, etc.	500 gm.
Red chillies	20 gm.
Coriander seeds	½ tsp.
Turmeric	a small piece or ¼ tsp. powder
Small red onions	4 bulbs
Garlic	4 flakes
Ginger	1.25 cm. (½") piece
Curry leaves	2 sprigs
Cocum (Kudampuli)	15—20 gm.
Salt	to taste
Coconut oil	30 ml.

1. Clean and cut fish into 2.5 cm. (1") slices or steaks. 2. Roast or dry heat red chillies, coriander seeds and turmeric. 3. Powder fine and grind to a smooth paste with onions and garlic. 4. Soak cocum in a little water. 5. Chop ginger into fine pieces. 6. In a heavy-bottomed stainless steel pan, first put in curry leaves and half the cocum, broken into small pieces. 7. Mix together the ground paste, fish and salt. 8. Arrange in the stainless steel pan with the remaining cocum pieces and chopped ginger. 9. Pour enough water to cover three-fourth fish. 10. Bring to boil on a quick fire and simmer till fish is tender. 11. Pour fresh coconut oil over it and remove from fire. 12. Cool and cover. This will keep for two days. If kept for longer period, reheat with a little water and a pinch of salt each day. Serves. 4.

10. Fish Curry (Madras)

Pomfret or surmai or mullet	1 (500 gm.)
Red chillies (use Sankeshwari or Kashmiri chillies)	10 gm.
Peppercorns	½ tsp.
Cumin seeds	1 gm.
Garlic	4—6 gm.
Onions	250 gm.
Tamarind	size of a lemon

Turmeric	2 gm.	*Fenugreek seeds*	5 gm.
Coriander seeds	10 gm.	*Tomatoes*	150 gm.
Oil	50 ml.	*Salt*	to taste
Cocunut	½	*Curry leaves*	a few
Green chillies	4—6 gm.		

1. Clean and slice the fish. 2. Grate coconut. Set aside one tbsp. for grinding and prepare two extracts of coconut milk with the remaining—the first thick (one cup), and the second thin (two cups). 3. Grind red chillies, coriander seeds and turmeric to a fine paste. 4. Grind coconut separately and half the onions. Slice the remaining onions. 5. Grind together garlic, peppercorns and cumin seeds. 6. Soak tamarind, in one cup of water. Squeeze out pulp, strain. 7. Chop tomatoes. 8. Heat oil. Add fenugreek seeds, curry leaves, sliced onions. Sauté. Add chopped tomatoes. Add the first lot of ground ingredients. Fry well. 9. Add ground coconut, onions, garlic, peppercorns and cumin seeds. Sauté. 10. Add second extract of coconut milk, tamarind juice and salt. Bring to boil. 11. Add fish. Simmer till the fish is done. 12. Add first extract of coconut milk. Test for seasoning. Bring to boil and remove.

Serves 4.

11. Prawns in Garlic Chilli Sauce

Prawns	500 gm.	*Red chillies*	7—8
Turmeric	¼ tsp.	*Tomatoes*	250 gm.
Garlic	5 flakes	*Vinegar*	50 ml.
Ginger	½" piece	*Oil*	1 tbsp.
Cumin	1½ tsp.	*Salt*	to taste

1. Clean prawns. 2. Grind spices using vinegar. 3. Heat oil. Fry spices. Add prawns, blanched tomatoes and

salt. 4. Bring to boil. Simmer till done. 5. Add vinegar as desired before removing from fire.

Serves 6.

12. Prawn Caldeen

Prawns	*2 kg.*	*Ginger*	*2.5 cm. (1") piece*
Lady's fingers	*500 gm.*	*Green chillies*	*30 gm.*
Coconuts	*2*	*Turmeric*	*½ tsp.*
Garlic	*10 flakes*	*Lime*	*½*
Onions	*250 gm.*	*Coconut oil*	*150 ml.*
Tamarind	*50 gm.*	*Salt*	*to taste*

1. Shell the prawns. Remove intestines. Wash well with salt and lime. 2. Slit green chillies. Slice ginger, garlic and onions. 3. Grate and grind coconuts to a fine paste. 4. Heat oil. Add sliced onions and sauté without discolouration. 5. Add coconut, and sliced garlic, ginger, green chillies and turmeric. 6. Add prawns and enough water to cook prawns. Cook on a slow fire. 7. Wipe lady's fingers with a damp cloth and cut into 5 cm. (2") pieces. 8. When prawns are half-cooked add tamarind juice and lady's fingers. Simmer till done.

Serves 20.

N.B. If desired lady's fingers can be fried in a little oil before adding them to the prawns.

13. Prawn Nissa

Tiger prawns (shelled)	*16*	*Oil*	*50 ml.*
Curd	*50 ml.*	*Salt*	*10 gm.*
Garam masala powder	*50 gm.*	*Chana powder*	
Yellow chilli powder	*50 gm.*	*(roasted)*	*10 gm.*
Ginger-garlic paste	*25 gm.*	*Yellow colour*	*as required*

Ajwain (crushed)	10 gm.	Chaat masala	
Lemon juice	10 ml.	powder	to taste

1. Hang the curd for two hours to drain out the whey. 2. Beat the curd and mix it with all the ingredients except prawns and chaat masala powder. 3. Marinate the cleaned prawns in the mixture overnight. 4. Thread the prawns on to a skewer and grill over charcoal till cooked. 5. Sprinkle chaat masala powder and squeeze lemon juice over the prawns and serve hot on a plate decorated with sliced tomatoes and cucumber and shredded onions, capsicum and beetroot.

Serves 4.

14. Lobster Masala

Lobsters (large)	2	Tomatoes	250 gm.
or lobster meat	500 gm.	Bay leaf (for flavour)	1
Red chillies	10 gm.	Cloves	2
Garlic	10 gm.	Cardamoms	2
Ginger	10 gm.	Peppercorns	5
Cumin	1 tsp.	Onions	150 gm.
Mustard seeds	1 tsp.	Oil	150 ml.
Turmeric	a large pinch	Salt	to taste

1. Grind together red chillies, garlic, ginger, cumin, mustard seeds, turmeric, peppercorns, cloves, cardamoms and onions (all the spices). 2. Heat the oil, add bay leaf and fry spices till oil floats on top. 3. Then put in lobster meat and chopped tomatoes. Add salt. Cook slowly without water till done. If necessary, sprinkle a little water.

Serves 4.

MEAT

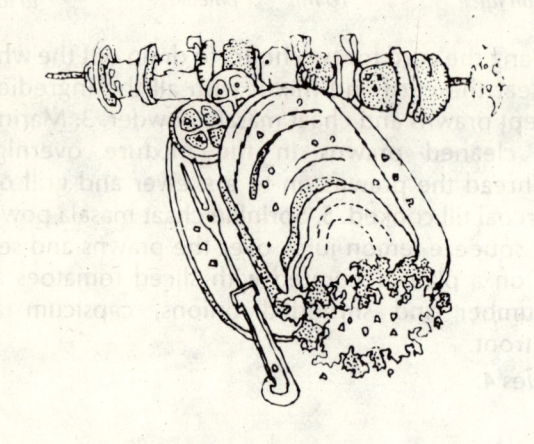

1. Mutton Baffat

Mutton	500 gm.	Groundnuts	5 gm.
Radish	150 gm.	Poppy seeds	5 gm.
Lime	¼	Green chillies	2
Split Bengal gram	5 gm.	Red chillies	5 gm.
Ginger	a small piece	Coconut	½
Garlic	a few flakes	Onion	55 gm.
Cloves	2	Fat	15 gm.
Cinnamon	a small piece	Salt	to taste
Peppercorns	a few	Vinegar	15 ml.
Turmeric	a pinch		

1. Clean and cut meat into 2.5 cm. (1") pieces. 2. Boil radish in lime water till tender. 3. Grind together turmeric, red chillies, ginger, garlic, poppy seeds, gram, groundnuts, cinnamon, cloves and peppercorns, using a little vinegar. 4. Make two extracts of coconut milk, the first one thick and the second

medium. 5. Heat fat. Add sliced onion and brown. 6. Add green chillies (whole), spices and meat and second extract of coconut milk, vinegar and salt. 7. Cook till meat is tender. Add cooked radish and first extract of coconut milk. 8. Temper with a few slices of onion fried in fat and serve hot.

Serves 4.

2. Mutton Khorma

Mutton	*500 gm.*	*Poppy seeds*	*10 gm.*
Dry coconut	*30 gm.*	*Green chillies*	*2*
Onions	*115 gm.*	*Cinnamon*	*2 gm.*
Ginger	*5 gm.*	*Cloves*	*2 gm.*
Garlic	*a few flakes*	*Peppercorns*	*2 gm.*
Red chillies	*5 gm.*	*Cardamoms*	*2 gm.*
Curd	*115 gm.*	*Fat*	*50 gm.*
Coriander powder	*15 gm.*		

1. Wash and cut meat. 2. Soak in curd for half an hour. 3. Grind together poppy seeds, dry coconut, garlic, ginger, coriander powder, red chillies (seeds removed), green chillies and half the onions. 4. Heat fat, fry remaining onions, sliced. 5. Add ground spices and meat. Fry for about 15 minutes. 6. Add remaining curd and tepid water and cook till meat is tender. 7. Add cinnamon, clove, peppercorns and cardamoms, roasted and powdered. 8. Cook for 5 to 10 minutes and serve hot.

Serves 4.

Culinary Cue: To make meat soft and tender, soak it in a small quantity of curd or vinegar for a few hours before cooking. This will also enhance the protein value of the meal.

3. Green Curry (Meat, Chicken or Liver)

Meat	680 gm.	Ginger	5 cm. (2") piece
Coconut	¼	Garlic	8—10 cloves
Coriander leaves	1 bunch	Turmeric	5 cm. (2") piece
Onions	2	Fennel	a little
Salt	to taste	Green chillies	6 large
Lemon	½—1	Potatoes if required	
Fat or oil	60 gm.		

1. Grind coconut to a thick paste. By adding water, extract about half a glass of milk. 2. Grind three green chillies, fennel, turmeric, seven to eight garlic cloves, half the ginger and some coriander leaves to a fine paste. 3. Chop remaining green chillies, ginger and coriander leaves and keep aside. 4. Heat fat and add two to three bruised cloves of garlic, then onions chopped fine, and cook till soft. 5. Add meat, salt and chopped chillies, ginger and coriander leaves. 6. When water has evaporated, pour in coconut milk and a little water and cook till tender. Boiled potatoes, peeled and diced, may be added. 7. Serve with cut lemon.

Serves 6.

4. Shahi Khorma

Mutton	500 gm.	Fat	50 gm.
Onions	200 gm.	Coconut	55 gm.
Poppy seeds	10 gm.	Curd	115 gm
Almonds	5 gm.	Garlic	2 cloves
Coriander seeds	15 gm.	Cloves	2 gm.
Ginger	a small piece	Cinnamon	2 gm.
Kashmiri chillies	10 gm.	Cardamoms	2 gm.
Cumin	a pinch	Dried milk	5 gm.
Sultanas	5 gm.	Salt	to taste

1. Wash and cut meat into 2.5 cm. (1") pieces. Grind poppy seeds, cumin, coriander seeds, ginger and garlic. 2. Remove seeds from red chillies. Soak in water and grind to a fine paste. 3. Grate coconut and extract milk. 4. Soak dry fruit and nuts in water. 5. Heat fat. Fry sliced onions, cloves, cinnamon and cardamoms, then the ground spices. 6. Add meat and fry. Add beaten curd, water and salt; cook till meat is tender. 7. Add coconut milk, dried milk sultanas, and almonds. Simmer for a few minutes. Remove. Serve hot.

Serves 4.

5. Mutton Bhopla

Mutton	250 gm.	*Chilli powder*	4 gm.
Red pumpkin	250 gm.	*Turmeric*	4 gm.
Green chillies	4 gm. (2)	*Garlic*	6 gm.
Curd	150 gm.	*Bay leaf*	1
Onions	150 gm.	*Ginger*	10 gm.
Garam masala powder		*Coriander leaves*	⅛ bunch
(cinnamon, cloves,		*Salt*	to taste
pepper, cumin)	4 gm.	*Fat*	30 gm.

1. Clean mutton, cut into 2.5 cm. (1") pieces. 2. Soak mutton in curd and salt for about one hour. 3. Grind together onions, ginger, garlic, turmeric and chilli powder. 4. Heat fat. Fry ground ingredients till rich brown in colour, and till fat starts oozing out. Add garam masala. 5. Add bay leaf, green chillies (whole) and mutton soaked in curd. Fry till mutton becomes rich brown in colour. 6. Add water and simmer till mutton becomes tender. 7. Meanwhile peel, boil and mash pumpkin. Add to the mutton when it is tender and cook till the gravy is very thick. 8. Garnish with chopped coriander leaves and serve hot.

6. Raan-E-Noorjahan

Baby lamb legs	2	Coriander seeds	10 gm.
Tomatoes	250 gm.	Ginger paste	10 gm.
Onions (chopped)	250 gm.	Garlic paste	10 gm.
Cinnamon	5 gm.	Refined oil	20 ml.
Cardamoms	5 gm.	Salt	to taste
Cloves	5 gm.	Pepper	to taste
Peppercorns	5 gm.	Cream	100 ml.
Bay leaves	5 gm.	Butter	50 gm.
Whole red chillies	5 gm.	Brandy	60 ml.
Aniseed	5 gm.	Dry fruits	10 gm.

1. Heat oil in a pan and sauté the chopped onions, ginger-garlic pastes, whole red chillies, aniseed, coriander seeds and whole garam masala together. When the spices are thoroughly browned, add the lamb legs and sauté. Add tomatoes and cook for some time. 3. Add water (4 litres) and simmer for two hours. 4. Remove lamb legs from gravy and strain the gravy. Cut the lamb legs into pieces and retain the bones to decorate the platter. 5. Cook the meat pieces in the strained gravy, season with salt and pepper and finish off with cream. 6. Arrange with gravy on platter around the bones, and decorate with silver foil. 7. Decorate the platter with tomato and cucumber slices, shredded onion, capsicum and beetroot. Sprinkle chopped dry fruits over.

Serves 4.

7. Country Captain

Mutton	500 gm.	Ginger	5 gm.
Onions	115 gm.	Potatoes	225 gm.
Sugar	a pinch	Coriander seeds	5 gm.

Vinegar	*10 ml.*	*Cumin seeds*	*a pinch*
Kashmiri chillies	*5 gm.*	*Turmeric*	*a pinch*
Green chillies	*5 gm.*	*Coriander leaves*	*¼ bunch*
Salt	*to taste*	*Fat*	*30 gm.*

1. Clean, wash and cut meat. 2. Chop onions and fry. 3. Add meat; fry lightly. 4. Add hot water and salt and cook. 5. Boil potatoes; slice and fry brown. 6. When meat is cooked, remove. To ground Kashmiri chillies, cumin and coriander seeds, and turmeric, add chopped ginger, green chillies and coriander leaves. 7. Add vinegar and sugar and cook till gravy is thick. 8. Add meat and potatoes. Cook for a few minutes longer and remove. Serve meat and gravy with potatoes on top.

Serves 4.

8. Mutton Curry (Mild)

Mutton	*500 gm.*	*Coconut*	*30 gm.*
Coriander powder	*10 gm.*	*Garam masala*	*a pinch*
Poppy seeds	*5 gm.*	*Onion*	*1*
Turmeric	*¼ tsp.*	*Vinegar*	*1 tsp.*
Ginger	*2.5 cm. (1") piece*	*Oil*	*25 ml.*
Garlic	*3 flakes*	*Salt*	*to taste*
Cashewnuts	*15 gm.*		

1. Clean and cut mutton into 2.5 cm. (1") pieces. 2. Grind together the spices, cashewnuts, and coconut. 3. Slice onion. Heat oil. Fry onion till crisp brown. 4. Add ground spices and fry for two to three minutes. 5. Add mutton. Fry for a further five minutes. Add salt. 6. Cover pan. Cook over very slow fire. Keep a little water over the lid of the pan to prevent meat from

burning. 7. Add hot water as desired, a little at a time till meat is tender. 8. Add vinegar. Check for seasoning. Remove.

Serves 4.

9. Roganjosh

Leg of mutton	500 gm.	Coriander powder	10 gm.
Tomatoes	115 gm.	Saltpetre	5 gm.
Fat	30 gm.	Mace	a pinch
Kashmiri chillies		Garlic	a few flakes
(without seeds)	15 gm.	Onions	115 gm.
Ginger	10 gm.	Rattan jog	a small piece
Nutmeg	a pinch	Salt	to taste
Saffron	a pinch	Stock	
Cumin	a pinch	Milk	enough to dissolve saffron

1. Clean and cut meat into 2.5 cm. (1") pieces with bones. 2. Chop onions. Grind Kashmiri chillies, coriander powder, ginger, cumin and garlic. 3. Heat fat. Fry onions, add ground spices and fry well. Add tomatoes. 4. Add meat, saltpetre and half of the saffron. 5. Fry for about five minutes. Add stock, nutmeg, mace, salt and rattan jog. 6. Cook gently till meat is tender. 7. When meat is cooked, add the rest of the saffron dissolved in a little milk.

Serves 4.

10. Safed Mas

Lamb	1 kg.	Black pepper	1 dsp. (20 gm.)
Curd	1½ cup (225 gm.)	Cumin	3 gm.
Fat	250 gm.	Poppy seeds	45 gm.

Onions	*150 gm.*	*Cashewnuts*	*25 gm.*
Garlic	*6 cloves*	*Salt*	*to taste*
Red chillies	*7 gm.*	*Water*	*½ litre*

1. Clean and cut lamb into 2.5 cm. (1") pieces with the bones. 2. Slice onions and garlic. 3. Grind together remaining spices and nuts. 4. Place all ingredients in a pressure cooker. 5. Cover and allow the steam to come up (for about 10 minutes). 6. Place 10 lb. pressure on. Cook for a further 15 minutes. Cool pressure cooker slowly. 7. Open lid and take out the curry.

Serves 10.

11. Meat and Coconut Fry (Iraichi Ulathiyathu)

Beef or mutton	*500 gm.*	*Peppercorns*	*½ tsp.*
Coconut	*115 gm. (½)*	*Small onion*	*10 gm.*
Coriander seeds	*30 gm.*	*Garlic*	*6 flakes*
Red chillies	*5—7*	*Ginger*	*1.25 cm. (½") piece*
Turmeric	*¼ tsp. or a small piece*	*Curry leaves*	*2 sprigs*
		Salt	*to taste*
Cinnamon	*½ tsp.*	*Coconut oil*	*50 ml.*
Cloves	*½ tsp.*		

1. Slice coconut into thin 1.25 cm. (½") pieces. Sprinkle a little turmeric powder. 2. Heat half the oil. Sauté coconut. Remove. 3. Clean and cut meat into 1.25 cm. (½") pieces. 4. Roast and powder fine coriander seeds, red chillies and turmeric. 5. Powder cinnamon, cloves and peppercorns. 6. Roast onions and garlic and grind to a fine paste. 7. Slice ginger. 8. Mix together meat, prepared spices, ground onions and garlic, ginger, curry leaves, coconut and salt with enough water to cook meat dry. 9. Keep on fire. Bring to boil quickly.

Reduce heat and cook over a gentle heat till tender. Cover tight so that no steam escapes. 10. When meat is tender and all water has evaporated, stir well and remove. 11. Heat remaining oil. Add meat and fry well.
Serves 4.

12. Mutton Jhal Faraizi

Mutton (roasted and cooled)	500 gm.	Fat	50 gm.
Pepper	1 tsp.	Potatoes	450 gm.
Red chillies	10 gm.	Onions	450 gm.
Salt	15 gm.		

1. Boil potatoes. Peel, cool and dice. 2. Dice roast meat into even portions. 3. Chop onions. 4. Grind together chillies and pepper. 5. Heat fat, fry onions lightly. Add meat, potatoes, ground spices and salt. 6. Fry on a slow fire till almost dry.
Serves 4.

13. Salli Ka Gosht

Potato juliennes, deep fried	20 gm.	Green chilli paste	5 gm.
Mutton (boneless)	600 gm.	Coriander leaves	20 gm.
Butter	50 gm.	Ginger-garlic paste	10 gm.
Onions (chopped)	2	Salt	to taste
Curd	250 gm.	Pepper	to taste
Cashewnut paste	20 gm.	Garam masala powder	10 gm.
Cream	250 ml.	Kasoori methi	5 gm.
		Nutmeg (grated)	2 gm.

1. Melt the butter and sauté onions till golden brown. 2. Add the mutton, ginger-garlic paste, chilli paste, garam masala powder, kasoori methi, curd, salt, pepper, grated nutmeg and cashewnut paste. Cook till

meat is tender. 3. Finish off with cream. 4. Garnish with chopped coriander leaves and juliennes of potato.

Serves 6.

14. Ball Curry (Malabar)

Meat (without bones)	250 gm.	*Peppercorns*	6
Green chillies	2	*Fennel*	½ tsp.
Onion	40 gm.	*Tomato*	1
Ginger	2.5 cm. (½") piece	*Coconut*	½
Salt	to taste	*Water for grinding spices and preparation of coconut milk*	2 cups
For curry			
Red chillies	4 gm.		
Coriander seeds	5 gm.	Tempering	
Ginger	1.25 cm. (½") piece	*Coconut oil*	10 ml.
Garlic	4 flakes (3 gm.)	*Ghee*	10 gm.
Turmeric	⅛ tsp. (½ gm.)	*Curry leaves*	a few sprigs
Cloves	3	*Red onion (2 pods)*	15 gm.
Cinnamon	1.25 cm. (½") piece	*Mustard seeds*	a pinch
		Cardamoms	2

1. Mince meat with the first lot of ingredients. Add salt and form into eight balls. 2. Roast red chillies and coriander seeds. Grind together with remaining spices. 3. Grate coconut and extract milk, first thick, second, after grinding, thinner. 4. Heat oil and ghee. Add mustard seeds. As seeds crackle, add curry leaves and sliced onions. When onions brown, add ground spices. 5. Fry for a further 5 to 10 minutes. 6. Add second extract of coconut milk. Bring to boil. Add blanched tomato. 7. Add meat balls one by one to simmering liquid. 8. Cook over very slow fire for about 20 minutes. 9. Add first extract of coconut milk. Bring to boil. Test for seasoning and remove.

Serves 4.

N.B. Instead of tomato, vinegar may be used.

15. Hyderabadi Kheema

Mutton	500 gm.	Potatoes	115 gm.
Tomatoes	450 gm.	Onions	115 gm.
Ginger	2.5 cm. (1") piece	Curd	55 gm.
Garlic	3 flakes	Fat	30 gm.
Green chillies	5	Salt	to taste
Garam masala	a pinch		

1. Clean and mince mutton. 2. Mince onions, garlic and ginger. Chop green chillies. 3. Heat fat. Fry ground garam masala, ginger, garlic, onions and green chillies. 4. Add meat and fry for a few minutes. 5. Add cut tomatoes and cook covered on slow fire. 6. Sprinkle a little water occasionally. 7. When almost cooked add diced potatoes, salt, and beaten curd. 8. Cook till potatoes are quite soft. Remove and serve hot.
Serves 4.

16. Shami Kababs

Bengal gram	55 gm.	Cumin powder	a pinch
Mutton	500 gm.	Cinnamon powder	a pinch
Onion	55 gm.	Lime rind (grated)	a little
Green chillies	10 gm.	Egg	1
Garlic	a few flakes	Fat to fry	30 gm.
Ginger	a small piece	Salt	10 gm.
Pepper	to taste	Coriander leaves	½ bunch
Coriander powder	10 gm.	Onion rings to decorate	
Turmeric	a pinch		

1. Soak gram for two to three hours. 2. Clean and cut mutton. 3. Boil together meat and gram and mince. 4. Chop half of the onions, garlic, ginger, green chillies and coriander leaves. 5. Grind remainder. 6. Mix

together minced meat, salt, all spices except chopped ones; grind to a paste. 7. Bind with egg. Divide mixture into equal portions. 8. Place chopped spices and grated lime rind in the centre, form into balls. Flatten and shallow fry till brown. 9. Serve garnished with rounds of raw onion and chopped coriander leaves.
Serves 4.

17. Grilled Spare Ribs

Spare ribs (pork)	1.5 kg.	Curd	390 ml.
Green chillies	20 gm.	Chilli powder	5 gm.
Ginger	10 gm.	Kashmiri chilli	
Garlic	10 gm.	powder	5 gm.
Papaya (green)	5 gm.	Salad oil	15 ml.
Lime	½	Orange colour	3 gm.
		Salt	to taste

1. Grind together green chillies, ginger and garlic. Grind papaya separately. 2. Beat curd, add ground ingredients and the chilli powders. Beat well. 3. Add salad oil and colouring and pass through a fine sieve. Cut spare ribs into 10 cm. (4") pieces lengthwise along the bone. 4. Apply lime and salt and set aside for 10 minutes. Then marinate in prepared batter for about two to three hours. Grill slowly over charcoal on a grid and turn occasionally to develop attractive colour and special flavour.
Serves 10.

18. Masala Trotters (Paya)

Trotters (cleaned)	1 doz.	Coconut	½
Red chillies	10	Cinnamon	2.5 cm. (1") piece

MEAT

Ginger	2.5 cm. (1") piece	Cloves	8
Garlic	8 cloves	Cardamoms	8
Salt	to taste	Coriander leaves	a few sprigs
Turmeric	¾ tsp.	Onions	4
Fat	2 tsp.	Coriander-cumin	
Chilli powder	½ tsp.	powder	1 tsp.
		Rice flour to wash	
		trotters	2—3 tsp.

1. Wash trotters using rice flour to rub in. 2. Boil washed trotters in a cooker for 20 to 25 minutes with five cups of water. 3. Grind red chillies, coconut, ginger, garlic, cinnamon, coriander seeds, cumin, cloves, cardamoms, turmeric powder, chilli powder and coriander leaves to a fine paste. 4. Fry sliced onions in fat and remove. 5. In the same fat, fry spices to a golden brown colour. 6. Add fried onions, spices and salt to trotters and simmer till the gravy is thick. Serves 6.

19. Kheema Kaleji

Minced meat	500 gm.	Sankeshwari	
Liver	1 kg.	chillies	about 5 gm.
Ginger	20 gm.	Coriander leaves	½ bunch
Garlic	1 pod	Green chillies	10 gm.
Cumin	2 gm.	Oil	100 ml.
Ajwain	2 gm.	Turmeric	¼ tsp.
Tomatoes	250 gm.	Onion (large)	1
Salt	to taste		

1. Grind together ginger and garlic. Finely chop coriander leaves. 2. Grind red chillies into a paste. 3. Slit green chillies. Slice onion. 4. Clean and cube liver. 5. Heat half the oil. Brown sliced onion and

remove, and grind to a paste. 6. Heat oil and lightly fry red chilli paste, ground ginger and garlic, cumin, ajwain, slit green chillies, turmeric, minced meat and liver. 7. Add ground browned onion. Fry for a few minutes. 8. Add salt, chopped tomatoes and cook over slow fire.

Serves 5.

POULTRY

1. Rogini Chicken

Chicken	1	*Cashewnuts*	30 gm.
Curd	250 gm.	*Poppy seeds*	15 gm.
Fat	100 gm.	*Onions (sliced and*	
For grinding		*browned)*	100 gm. (1)
Kashmiri red chillies		*Garlic*	6—8 flakes
(without seeds)	7 gm.	*Ginger*	2.5 cm. (1") piece

1. Joint chicken. Brown in fat. Do not overfry. Remove. 2. Fry ground spices over slow fire till the fat floats on top. Add chicken. 3. Stir well and cook gently, sprinkling a little water if necessary. 4. When three fourths done, beat curd into a smooth paste and pour over the chicken. 5. Cook again till chicken is tender. Do not stir. 6. Garnish with coriander leaves if desired. Serves 6 to 8.

N.B. Fat can be reduced by as much as 50 gm. if you do not want the dish to be too rich.

2. Chicken Curry

Chicken	1 (about 1.35 kg.)	For grinding	
Onions	225 gm.	*Coriander powder*	15 gm.
Garlic	6 flakes	*Peppercorns*	6
Salt	to taste	*Ginger*	10 gm.
Lime	1	*Red chillies*	5
Fat	30 gm.	*Poppy seeds*	1 tsp.
		Cumin	½ tsp.
		Grated coconut	55 gm. (¼)

1. Clean, wash and joint chicken. 2. Slice onions and garlic. 3. Heat fat. Add onions and fry. Add the chicken pieces and brown well. 4. Add sliced garlic and ground spices. Fry for two or three minutes. 5. Add water and salt and simmer till chicken is tender and gravy is thick. 6. Add lime juice just before serving.

Serves 6.

3. Chicken Chacouti

Chicken	1	*Garlic*	5 flakes
Coconut	1	*Kashmiri chillies*	12
Coriander seeds	30 gm.	*Onions*	5 (large)
Cumin	1 tsp.	*Turmeric*	2.5 cm. (1") piece
Poppy seeds	1½ tbsp.	*Vinegar*	½ cup.
Cardamoms	3	*Tamarind*	5 gm.
Cinnamon	2 gm.	*Bay leaves*	a few
Cloves	2 gm.	*Mace*	a small piece
Ginger	3.5 cm. (1½") piece	*Badyani*	
Mustard seeds	5 gm.	(star anise)	a small piece
Peppercorns	2 gm.	*Salt*	to taste

1. Clean and joint the chicken. Apply salt. 2. Chop one onion, apply it to the chicken with vinegar and keep aside. Slice ginger. 3. Fry all spices (except cumin, garlic and mustard seeds) in a little oil till coriander seeds become golden brown, then add cumin, garlic and mustard seeds and remove. 4. Slice one onion and sauté till soft. Grate coconut and roast till light brown. 5. Grind spices with fried onions to a fine paste. Grind coconut coarsely, separately. 6. Fry remaining onions, add chicken and fry, then add spices, coconut, tamarind water and salt and a little water; allow to cook on slow fire till done.

Serves 6.

4. Chicken Khorma

Chicken	1 (about 1 kg.)	Coriander seeds	10 gm.
Coconut	1	Onions	750 gm.
Poppy seeds	100 gm.	Salt	to taste
Cashewnuts	100 gm.	Curd	500 gm.
Red chillies	1—2	Fat	50 gm.
Green chilli	1		

1. Clean and joint chicken. Grind together coconut, poppy seeds, cashewnuts, red chilli, green chilli, coriander seeds and half the onions. 2. Heat fat and lightly sauté remaining onions (sliced). 3. Add ground ingredients and fry for a few minutes. 4. Add jointed chicken. Fry for a further 5 minutes. Add salt to taste and beaten curd. 5. Cook over low fire till done.

Serves 6.

Culinary Cue: Cooking poultry on a high temperature destroys valuable nutrients. Always use low or medium heat.

5. Chicken Mulligutwanny Curry (Mild)

Chicken	1 kg.	Fennel	3 gm.
Small onions (sliced)	115 gm.	Peppercorns	20
Garlic (sliced)	6 flakes	Split Bengal gram	10 gm.
Ginger (sliced)	2.5 cm. (1") piece	Turmeric	¼ tsp.
		Coconut	½
Cinnamon	a small piece	Lime	1
Tomatoes	225 gm.	*Tempering*	
Curry leaves	a few	Clarified butter	10 gm.
Salt	2 tsp.	Red onion	1
Kashmiri chillies	2	Curry leaves	a few
Coriander seeds	10 gm.		
Cumin	a small pinch		

1. Joint the chicken and simmer gently with the next seven ingredients for about 10 minutes. 2. Roast red chillies and Bengal gram separately. Grind together the next seven ingredients, from Kashmiri chillies to turmeric, to a smooth paste. 3. Make two extracts of coconut milk. Add second extract and ground spices to chicken and cook till tender. 4. Add first extract of coconut milk and bring to boil. Remove. 5. Add lime juice. Temper.

Serves 6.

6. Fried Chicken

Dressed chicken	1 kg.	Peppercorns	1 gm.
Kashmiri red chillies (remove seeds)	6 gm.	Curry leaves	1 sprig
		Cinnamon and cloves	1 gm.
Sankeshwari red chillies	4 gm.	Oil	50 ml.
Red onion	30 gm.	Salt	to taste
Garlic	5 gm.		

1. Clean and joint the chicken into eight pieces. Wash

well and drain. 2. Grind together the remaining ingredients (except oil and curry leaves) with salt. Apply on chicken ensuring that the spices are rubbed well into the chicken, especially the inner parts. 3. Place in a pan, add a cup of water (200 ml.) and the curry leaves and bring to boil. Simmer till chicken is tender and dry. 4. Heat oil in a frying pan. Add chicken pieces and fry over medium heat tossing the chicken pieces. Do not overfry.

Serves 6.

Culinary Cue: Your chicken will look a rich golden brown if you add a few drops of yellow food colouring to the oil in which it is fried.

7. Chicken Temperado

Chicken	1 (small)	*Cloves*	4
Red chillies	4	*Salt*	to taste
Tamarind	a very small ball	For grinding	
Vinegar	3 dsp.	*Turmeric*	2.5 cm. (1") piece
Sugar	2 tsp.	*Ginger*	2.5 cm. (1") piece
Onion	1 (large)	*Peppercorns*	12
Oil	4—6 dsp.	*Cinnamon*	a small piece
Cumin	1 tsp.	*Cardamom*	1
Garlic	6 flakes		

1. Clean and joint the chicken, apply salt and set aside for about 20 minutes. 2. Slice onion, heat oil and fry onion till golden brown; add chicken pieces and let it cook for about 10 minutes with the lid on. 3. Add tamarind juice and continue cooking for another 15 minutes. 4. Crush cumin, garlic, cloves and add to the ground spices. 5. Add spices to the chicken, mix well; add chillies and a little water. Cook for 15 minutes.

8. Chicken Shahjahani

Chicken	1 kg.	Chilli powder	3 gm.
Onions	150 gm.	Coriander powder	2 gm.
Tomatoes	50 gm.	Turmeric	1 gm.
Cashewnuts	20 gm.	Fresh cream	30 gm.
Ginger	5 gm.	Coriander leaves	1 bunch
Garlic	5 gm.	Fat	50 gm.
Green chillies	10 gm.		

6. Add vinegar and sugar. Cook for 5 minutes and remove from fire.

Serves 6.

1. Slice onions and fry till light brown. 2. Grind ginger, garlic and green chillies to a smooth paste and add it to the onions. 3. Add powdered masalas, fry well. 4. Add the chicken pieces and fry. 5. Add chopped tomatoes and chopped coriander leaves. 6. Add a cup of water and simmer till chicken pieces are tender. 7. Soak cashewnuts in half a cup of hot water. Drain and grind to a smooth paste. 8. Serve chicken with cashewnut paste and cream.

Serves 8.

9. Chicken Fry Coorg

Chicken	800 gm. (1)	Cumin	1 tsp.
Green chillies	12	Pepper	2 tsp.
Garlic	2 pods	Salt	to taste
Ginger	5 cm. (2") piece	Fat	50 gm.
Red onion	1 (large)	Vinegar	1 tbsp.

1. Grind spices and salt with vinegar. 2. Apply over jointed chicken. Set aside for one hour. 3. Heat fat.

Add chicken and fry over slow fire. 4. Cook covered till chicken is tender and fat floats on top.

Serves 6.

10. Buttered Tandoori Chicken (Chicken Makhanwala)

Chicken	1	Kashmiri chilli powder	10 gm.
Butter for batter	125 gm. (approx.)	Green chillies	20 gm.
		Ginger	10 gm.
Butter for basting	125 gm. (approx.)	Garlic	10 gm.

Tandoori masala
Hot red chilli powder   5 gm.

1. Grind tandoori masala and mix with butter. 2. Make incisions or slits on the breasts and legs of the chicken. 3. Marinate chicken in the mixture for 10-12 hours. 4. Bake in the tandoor, basting frequently with butter, till chicken is cooked; or remove when three-fourths done, fry in butter, return again to the tandoor for 3 to 4 minutes. Keep basting till done.

Serves 6.

N.B. To make murg makhani, prepare tandoori chicken, melt butter, sauté the leftover marinade in butter; pour over the chicken.

11. Chicken Cafreal

Chicken	1 (about 800 gm.)	Coconut vinegar	10 ml.
Ginger	20 gm.	Bancal sauce or	
Garlic	20 gm.	Worcester sauce	20 ml.
Green chillies	30 gm.	Tomato sauce	50 ml.
(remove seeds if desired)		Salt	to taste

Turmeric	5 gm.	Rum	10 ml.
Pepper	1 gm.	Oil to saute	10—20 ml.
Lime	1		

1. Clean chicken. 2. Prepare a paste of ginger-garlic and chillies. Add all the other ingredients except rum and oil. Apply over chicken and set aside for about one and half hours. 3. Cook in the oven for 20 minutes at 250°C—300°C. Remove, turn and cook for a further 15 minutes to 20 minutes in the oven. 4. Joint the chicken. Sauté in fat. Add rum when it is hot. Cook a little longer. 5. Garnish with sautéd potatoes (boiled), onions and tomatoes cooked in the same gravy.

Serves 6.

12. Kozhi Mulugu Veraval Chettinad

Chicken	1	Cumin (Jeera)	2 gm.
Small onions	6	Fenugreek (Methi)	2 gm.
Garlic	10 gm.	Salt	to taste
Tomatoes	1—2	Turmeric	¼ tsp.
Red chillies (Sankeshwari)	4	Cinnamon stick	1 piece
Black pepper	5 gm.	Coconut	¼
Fennel (Saunf)	5 gm.		

1. Skin, clean and cut chicken into 10 pieces. 2. Peel garlic and onion. 3. Roast chillies, black pepper and half the amount of fennel and cumin. 4. Pound to make a coarse powder. 5. Add sliced onion and garlic and pound with spices. 6. Heat oil in a frypan. Add whole fenugreek and fennel. Add roughly chopped tomatoes and fry for 2 to 3 minutes. 7. Add the chicken and fry well till brown. Add salt and turmeric. Add cinnamon stick. Cook on a slow fire till chicken is

three-fourth done. 8. Add ground coconut, ground ginger. Continue cooking till chicken is cooked and dry.

Serves 6.

13. Duck Roast

Plump duck	1 (about 1 kg.)	Oil	60 ml.
Ginger	2.5 cm. (1") piece	Onions	115 gm. (1)
Garlic	6 flakes	Tomatoes	225 gm.
Vinegar	2 tbsp.	Kashmiri red chillies or	
Salt	to taste	red chillies with	
Pepper	¼ tsp.	seeds removed	2
Butter	15 gm.	Sugar	¼ tsp.

1. Clean duck and keep it whole. 2. Grind ginger, garlic and pepper. 3. Apply on duck and prick with a fork to let spices seep in. 4. Marinate in vinegar for half an hour. 5. Heat butter and oil in a large strong-bottomed pan. 6. Add sliced onions, ground red chillies and chopped tomatoes. Add duck and brown. 7. Add two or three cups boiling water and salt. 8. Cook tightly covered till duck is tender. 9. Add sugar and remove from fire.

Serves 6.

N.B. This can be served with roasted or fried potatoes and boiled vegetables.

SWEETS

1. Balushai

Refined flour	115 gm.	Pistachio nuts	a few
Soda bicarb	a pinch	Fat to fry (absorption)	30 gm.
Fat	45 gm.	Syrup	
Curd	15 gm.	Sugar	115 gm.
Cold water to mix		Water	30 ml.
Cardamoms	2	Lime juice	a few drops

1. Sieve flour with salt and soda bicarb. 2. Add crushed cardamoms. Rub in fat and beaten curd. 3. Add cold water to make a soft dough. 4. Divide into equal-sized balls. 5. Flatten each ball between the palms so as to have the centre thinner than the sides. 6. Deep fry in hot fat on slow fire, leaving undisturbed for 10 minutes. 7. Turn over and repeat process. 8. When cooked, remove from fat and drain. 9. When quite cold, dip in prepared syrup and garnish with sliced

pistachio nuts. 10. To prepare syrup boil water and sugar and stir till dissolved. Cook to one string consistency, sprinkle lime juice.

Serves 4.

2. Chiroti

Refined flour	*200 gm.*	*Fat for frying*	
Rice flour	*30 gm.*	*(absorption)*	*50 gm.*
Fat	*115 gm.*	*Rice flour for*	
Sugar (powdered)	*100 gm.*	*dusting*	*50 gm.*
Salt	*a pinch*		

1. Sieve flour with salt, rub in half the fat. Make a dough as for puris using a little water (60 ml. for 22 pieces). 2. Cream rice flour and remaining fat. Leave in cold water. 3. Divide dough into small balls and roll into thin chapaties. 4. Take chapati, smear with the creamy mixture. Sprinkle over with a little rice flour and place another chapati on top of it. Smear again with cream and dust over with rice flour. 5. Roll and cut into pieces, roll slightly and deep fry. Sprinkle powdered sugar over, while it is still hot. 6. Repeat process.

Makes 25 chirotis.

3. Semiya Payasam

Vermicelli	*55 gm.*	*Saffron*	*a pinch*
Milk	*250 ml.*	*Sultanas*	*30 gm.*
Fat	*30 gm.*	*Cashewnuts*	*30 gm.*
Sugar	*55 gm.*	*Cardamoms*	*a few*

SWEETS 87

1. Heat fat. Fry vermicelli. 2. Add milk and bring to boil quickly. 3. Add sugar and remove from fire. 4. Fry cashewnuts and sultanas and add to payasam along with crushed cardamoms. Add saffron soaked in a little milk.

Serves 4.

4. Falooda

Milk	1 litre	Tukmeri or	
Cream	170 gm.	sabja seeds	4 tbsp
Rose syrup	300 ml.	Cornflour	60 gm.
Sugar	85 gm.		

1. Mix cornflour with a little cold milk to make a smooth paste. 2. Boil half the milk. Add half the sugar. 3. Pour over cornflour paste, stirring well. 4. Return to fire and cook till thick. 5. When thick remove and pass through a colander on to ice-cold water. 6. Meanwhile soak sabja seeds in cold water and allow them to swell up. 7. Pour a small quantity of rose syrup in six glasses. 8. Put in soaked sabja seeds and the cornflour globules. 9. Mix remaining milk and sugar and pour into the glasses. 10. Top with cream and serve cold with crushed ice cubes.

Serves 6.

5. Phirnee

Rice flour	30 gm.	Almonds or	
Sugar	60 gm.	cashewnuts	15 gm.
Milk	300 ml.	Pistachio nuts	10 gm.
Cardamom powder	a pinch		

1. Mix rice flour with a little cold milk. 2. Boil remaining milk. Add to rice flour mixture. 3. Cook on a slow fire till it becomes fairly thick. 4. Draw the pan to the side of the fire and sprinkle sugar. Place back on the fire. 5. When the sugar is dissolved and the contents are thick, remove from fire. Sprinkle with cardamom powder. 6. Pour into flat dishes (phirnee looks best if it is set in individual dishes). 7. Decorate with shredded nuts. Cool and serve.

Serves 4.

N.B. Silver paper may be used to decorate.

6. Doodh Kamal

Milk	*1 litre*	*Oranges*	*4*
Sugar	*50 gm.*	*Rose water*	*a few drops*

1. Boil milk to a third. Add sugar and rose water. 2. Peel oranges. Remove skin and seeds from each segment keeping the segment whole. 3. Pour milk into a glass bowl. Arrange segments of orange and chill. 4. Serve cold.

Serves 6.

7. Carrot Halwa

Carrots	*225 gm.*	*Hydrogenated fat or*	
Sugar	*115 gm.*	*clarified butter*	*55 gm.*
Milk	*120 ml.*	*Dried fruits and nuts*	*20 gm.*
Cardamoms	*a few*		

1. Wash carrots, scrape and grate. 2. Add carrots to milk and cook. 3. When milk dries up add fat and fry.

4. Add sugar, prepared dried fruits and crushed cardamoms.

Serves 4.

8. Bottle Gourd Halwa

Bottle gourd	450 gm.	Fat	115 gm.
Milk	250 ml.	Cardamoms	3
Sugar	340 gm.		

1. Peel and grate gourd. 2. Boil in milk; cook till all moisture is dried up. 3. Add sugar, fat and dry fruits and nuts if desired. 4. Fry for a few minutes. Sprinkle cardamom powder over.

Serves 4.

9. Wheat Halwa (White)

Whole wheat	1 kg.	Vegetable shortening	450 gm.
or wheat flour	450 gm.	Pure ghee	225 gm.
Sugar	1.8 kg.	Cashewnuts	225 gm.
Milk	1.2 litres (2 bottles)	Cardamoms	10 gm.
Water	4.75 litres (8 bottles)		

1. Soak wheat in water for about 16 hours. (Change water twice during soaking period.) 2. Grind in a round stone grinder. 3. Strain through a coarse jelly cloth. 4. If wheat flour is used, make a wet dough. Leave overnight. 5. Pass through a fine cloth. 6. Mix together the strained wheat, milk, water and sugar. 7. Cook till thick, stirring all the time. When thick, add fat and cashewnuts. 8. Continue cooking till a small portion rolled between thumb and forefinger forms a non-sticky ball. 9. Remove from fire. Add powdered

90 SWEETS

cardamoms. 10. Spread in flat, one-inch deep metal trays. Leave to cool. Cut into 5 cm. (2") pieces.
Serves 6.

10. Coconut Barfi

Mawa	*2.75 kg.*	*Coconut grated*	
Sugar	*1.35 kg.*	*fine and dried*	*340 gm.*
Pink or green colour if desired			

1. Mix sugar with mawa, place in a frying pan over gentle heat, and stir. 2. When mixture is ready (i.e. mixture forms balls when tested with fingers), remove from fire. Add coconut and stir well. 3. Spread on a greased tray (keeping a little aside). 4. Mix colouring in the portion set aside. (The colour should be light.) 5. Put back on fire. Cook till it becomes creamy. 6. Spread on top of the first layer. Allow to cool, cut into cubes.
Makes 100 pieces.

11. Cashewnut Barfi

Sugar	*300 gm.*	*Cardamoms*	*2 gm.*
Cashewnuts	*100 gm.*	*Fat*	*10 gm.*
Coconut	*150 gm.*		

1. Soak cashewnuts in water for one hour. 2. Grind coconut and cashewnuts into a fine paste. 3. Add sugar and cook the mixture on a slow fire stirring constantly. 4. Add fat and keep stirring until the mixture leaves the sides of the pan. 5. Add cardamom powder, remove the mixture, and pour on a greased plate for cooling.

6. When cold, cut into cubes.

Serves 4.

12. Boondi Ladoo

Gram flour	*115 gm.*	*Water*	*60 ml.*
Yellow colour	*5 gm.*	*Cardamoms*	*a few*
Soda bicarb	*a small pinch*	*Pistachios*	*5 gm.*
Sugar	*115 gm.*	*Fat (absorption)*	*30 gm.*

1. Make a thick batter with gram flour and soda bicarb dissolved in water. 2. Heat fat in a deep frying pan. 3. Drop batter through a perforated spoon. Fry for one or two minutes. 4. Prepare syrup with sugar and water to two string consistency. 5. Put fried boondi into syrup. Remove from syrup, add crushed cardamoms and pistachio nuts and form into balls. Colour can be added to the batter if required.

Serves 4.

13. Magaj

Bengal gram flour	*500 gm.*	*Pistachio nuts*	*10 gm.*
Sugar	*250 gm.*	*Cardamoms*	*5 gm.*
Mawa	*50 gm.*	*Fat*	*250 gm.*
Almonds	*10 gm.*		

1. Mix gram flour with half the fat and pass through a sieve. 2. Fry the mixture in the remaining fat till it browns. 3. Add mawa. Prepare sugar syrup (one string consistency). 4. Add sugar syrup and powdered cardamoms to the mixture. 5. Mix it well. Pour into a greased plate. 6. Decorate with almonds and pistachio nuts. 7. Mark diagonals. Leave to cool. Cut into cubes.

Serves 5.

14. Shahi Tukra

Bread slices	4	*Saffron*	*a pinch*
Sugar	*400 gm.*	*Cashewnuts*	*15 gm.*
Milk	*300 ml.*	*Pistachio nuts*	*15 gm.*
Cardamoms	2	*Fat*	*15 gm.*

1. Heat fat. Fry slices of bread. Remove. 2. Mix equal amount of water to milk and bring to boil. Add sugar and boil for 10 minutes. 3. Arrange the browned bread in the same pan without placing one slice on top of the other. 4. Heat saffron and soak in a little milk. Pour saffron on the slices of bread. 5. Cook on low heat till moisture is absorbed. 6. Garnish with chopped nuts and sprinkle with crushed cardamoms. Serve hot.

Serves 4.

15. Peanut Chikki

Jaggery	*170 gm.*	*Roasted peanuts*	*300 gm.*
Fat	*1 tsp.*	*Water*	*½ cup*

1. Remove skin of peanuts and crush them into large pieces. 2. Break jaggery. Add water and make a syrup. 3. To check the consistency of the syrup put a bit of it in cold water. If it can be rolled into a hard ball, (120°C/250°F), remove from fire. 4. Add nuts and mix well. 5. Pour into a greased plate, spread evenly and cut into pieces.

16. Gulab Jamun

Mawa	*75 gm.*	*Water*	*35 ml.*
Sugar	*75 gm.*	*Rose water*	*a few drops*

Cardamom powder	*a pinch*	*Soda bicarb*	*a small pinch*
Arrowroot	*10 gm.*	*Fat to fry*	

1. Prepare a syrup of one string consistency with water and sugar. Add the rose water. 2. Pass the mawa through a sieve. Add cardamom powder, sieved arrowroot and a little cold water in which the soda bicarb has been dissolved. 3. Make a soft dough without kneading. 4. Divide into equal portions and shape into small balls. 5. Fry in deep fat till light brown. The frying should be done on a very slow fire and the fat should be stirred constantly. 6. Remove, cool for a short while and put into the prepared cold syrup.

Makes 25 jamuns.

17. Shrikhand

Milk	*470 ml.*	*Pistachio nuts*	*5 gm.*
Curd	*15 ml.*	*Charoli nuts*	*5 gm.*
Powdered sugar	*115 gm.*	*Saffron*	*a pinch*
Cardamoms	*1—2*		

1. Boil milk and leave to cool. 2. When moderately hot add beaten curd. Mix well by pouring from one pan to another and back. 3. Keep aside covered for 10-12 hours. 4. Pour into a clean muslin cloth and tie loosely. 5. Hang the bag for two to three hours to let all liquid drip through. 6. Sprinkle crushed cardamoms and leave for one hour. 7. Tie a strong cloth over a pan. 8. Take small quantities of sugar and curd and mix well over the cloth. Put into a clean bowl. Continue till all the curd is mixed. 9. Add saffron. Mix well, garnish with sliced pistachios and charoli. Cool and serve.

Serves 4.

18. Thali Sweet

Semolina	*115 gm.*	*Sugar*	*225 gm.*
Almonds	*30 gm.*	*Whites of eggs*	*5*
Butter	*115 gm.*	*Rose water*	*½ wine glass*

1. Blanch and mince almonds. 2. Cream butter and sugar till fluffy and light. 3. Add semolina, mix well. Add minced almonds. 4. Beat egg whites stiff and fold in gradually. 5. Add rose water, mix well and leave aside for half an hour. 6. Put the mixture in a greased tin. Decorate the top with thin strips of kneaded flour. 7. Bake in a moderate oven.
Serves 4.

19. Mysore Pak

Bengal gram flour	*125 gm.*	*Cardamoms*	*5 gm.*
Sugar	*400 gm.*	*Water*	*100 ml.*
Fat	*600 gm.*		

1. Heat fat to boiling point. Remove and set aside. 2. Add water to sugar and prepare a syrup of three string consistency. 3. Take about 50 gm. of the fat and roast gram flour in it for two to three minutes. (Do not allow to brown.) 4. Sprinkle a little water on the gram flour to test whether it has been properly roasted in which case it will splutter. 5. Add sugar syrup to the roasted gram flour and stir well on fire. 6. Add gradually the remaining fat stirring continuously and vigorously till the fat starts floating on top of the mixture. 7. Remove from the fire and pour the mixture on to a tray. 8. Allow the tray to cool in a slanting position so that excess fat is drained off. 9. Sprinkle

crushed cardamoms and cut into diamond shapes. Makes 25 pieces.

20. Bibique

Coconuts	4	Egg yolks	20
Flour	3 cups (600 gm.)	Cardamom/Nutmeg	
Sugar	6 cups (1.2 kg.)	Ghee	½ cup

1. Extract thick juice of grated coconut. 2. Prepare sugar syrup (thick) with 6 cups water. Cool down. 3. Add beaten yolks and coconut milk and make into a thin batter (as for pancakes). Add flavouring. 4. Melt half a cup of ghee in a heavy-bottomed pan or pie dish and place it in an oven. 5. When hot, pour in about one to one and a half cups of the batter. Close the oven and cook for about 20-30 minutes or until brown on top. 6. Put a spoon of fat on top and pour another layer of batter. Bake for a further 20-30 minutes. 7. Repeat layer by layer till the batter is used up. When done, remove from fire, turn over and sprinkle icing sugar.

SNACKS

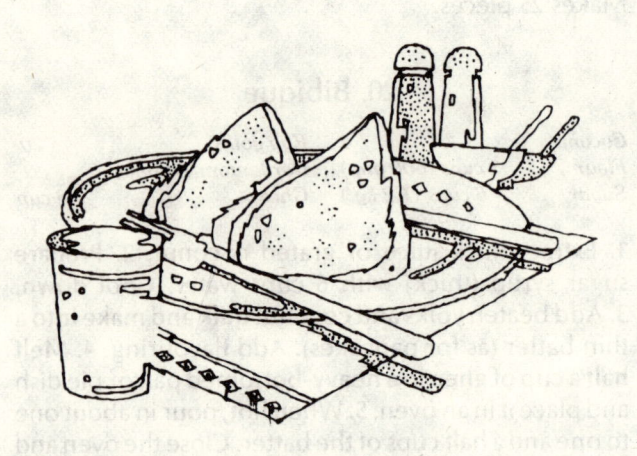

1. Masala Vada

Split red gram	*115 gm.*	*Salt*	*to taste*
Onion	*30 gm.*	*Prawns (boiled and*	
Green chillies	*2*	*seasoned)*	*10*
Red chillies	*2*		

1. Wash and soak gram for two hours. 2. Grind the gram coarsely (or pass through a mincer). 3. Mix with finely chopped onion and green chillies, coarsely ground red chillies, and salt. 4. Mix well together and shape into small flat rounds about 0.8 cm. (1/3") thick (10 pieces). 5. Place one prawn on top of each vada. 6. Deep fry till cooked and crisp.

Makes 10 vadas.

Culinary Cue: Fried food should always be put in a sieve lined with newspaper to retain their crispness.

2. Potato Bonda

Potatoes	500 gm.	Lime	½
Onions	125 gm.	Curry leaves	2 sprigs
Ginger	10 gm.	Bengal gram	
Green chillies	10 gm.	flour (besan)	60 gm.
Turmeric	1 gm.	Soda bicarb	1 gm.
Mustard seeds	2 gm.	Salt	10 gm.
Fat	10 gm.	Oil (absorption)	50 gm.

1. Boil and peel potatoes. Mash. 2. Chop onions, ginger, green chillies and curry leaves fine. 3. Heat fat and add mustard seeds. 4. When mustard seeds crackle, add chopped ingredients, potatoes, turmeric and salt. Add lime juice, mix well and remove from fire. 5. Divide into 20 portions (each the size of a large lime). 6. Dip in prepared batter and deep fry till golden brown. 7. Serve hot with tamarind chutney, or date and tamarind chutney.

BATTER

1. Sift together gram flour, soda bicarb and salt. 2. Add three-fourth cup water (75 ml.) and make a smooth batter of medium thickness.

Makes 20 bondas.

TAMARIND CHUTNEY

Tamarind	50 gm.	Chilli powder	2 gm.
Jaggery	10 gm.	Salt	5 gm.
Green chillies	2 gm.	Water	300 ml.

1. Soak tamarind in water and extract juice. 2. Mix all ingredients. Boil, strain and use.

DATE AND TAMARIND CHUTNEY

Dates	*75 gm.*	*Chilli powder*	*2 gm.*
Tamarind	*25 gm.*	*Salt*	*5 gm.*
Cumin	*2 gm.*	*Water*	*300 ml.*

1. Soak dates and tamarind in water for one hour. 2. Roast and powder cumin. 3. Remove seeds from tamarind and dates. 4. Mix all ingredients thoroughly in a blender.

3. Assorted Pakoras

Cauliflower	*225 gm.*	*Salt*	*to taste*
Brinjal	*225 gm.*	*Chilli powder*	*to taste*
Lady's fingers	*225 gm.*	*Bengal gram flour*	*125 gm.*
Onions	*225 gm.*	*Soda bicarb*	*a pinch*
Potatoes	*225 gm.*	*Water*	*to make batter*
Pumpkin	*225 gm.*		

1. Prepare a batter of pouring consistency using salt, chilli powder, gram flour and water. 2. Peel and cut pumpkin and potatoes into thin slices. Break cauliflower into flowerettes. Cut onions into rings. Season with salt and chilli powder. Slit lady's fingers from the sides and season lightly. 3. Dip in batter and fry in hot fat. 4. Serve hot with tomato chilli chutney. Serves 25.

TOMATO CHILLI CHUTNEY

Tomatoes	*300 gm.*	*Salt*	*10 gm.*
Red chillies	*10 gm.*		

1. Remove seeds from red chillies. 2. Soak in hot water. Drain. 3. Roast tomatoes in hot ash or over light flame. 4. Grind chillies and tomatoes with salt to a smooth paste.

4. Samosas (Plain)

Refined flour	500 gm.	*Potatoes*	1.5 kg.
Fat	115 gm.	*Green chillies*	30 gm.
Salt	50 gm.	*Lime*	1
Onions	500 gm.	*Turmeric*	a small pinch
Mustard seeds	5 gm.	*Oil to fry*	

1. Sift flour. Rub in fat. Add salt and cold water and make a fairly soft dough. 2. Set aside, covered, for at least half an hour. 3. Boil potatoes in their jackets. Peel and chop into small pieces. 4. Chop green chillies and onions fine. 5. Heat about 50 ml. of oil. Add mustard seeds. As they crackle, add potatoes, turmeric, chopped onions, green chillies and salt. 6. Mix well over fire. Add lime juice and remove. 7. Knead dough well. Divide dough into small portions. Roll out each portion to a round about 7.5 cm. (3") in diameter. 8. Cut down the centre. Make a cone of each portion. Put in prepared filling. 9. Seal edges with water. 10. Deep fry in fat till light brown. Serve hot.

Makes 80 samosas.

5. Cocktail Samosas with Liver Stuffing

Refined flour	115 gm.	*Worcestershire*	
Butter	70 gm.	*sauce*	1 tsp.
Chicken liver	225 gm.	*Salt*	to taste
Onions	100 gm.	*Fat*	to fry
Bacon	50 gm.		

1. Sift flour, add salt. Rub in fat. Add enough water to make a soft dough. 2. Knead well and set aside, covered, for at least half an hour. 3. Sauté chopped

onions and bacon in melted butter. 4. Add chicken liver cut into small pieces. 5. When cooked, add Worcestershire sauce and salt to taste. 6. Knead dough. Divide into small portions. 7. Roll out into rounds about 5 cm. (2") in diameter and paper thin. Cut down the centre 8. Make a cone of each piece. Put in prepared filling. 9. Seal the edges with water. 10. Deep fry in fat till light brown. 11. Serve hot.

Makes 15 Samosas.

6. Vegetable Puffs

Refined flour	115 gm.	*Coriander leaves*	*a few*
Fat	20 gm.	*Green chillies*	5 gm.
Salt	to taste	*Turmeric*	*a pinch*
Rice flour	1 tbsp.	*Chilli powder*	*a pinch*
Filling		*Cardamom powder*	*a little*
Potatoes	115 gm.	*Clove powder*	*a pinch*
Cauliflower	225 gm.	*Lime*	¼
Peas	115 gm.	*Salt*	*to taste*
Onions	115 gm.	*Fat to fry (absorption)*	30 gm.

1. Mix flour and salt. 2. Rub one portion of fat in flour, knead with water to a soft dough. 3. Divide the dough into even number of portions, roll into thin rounds. 4. Make a paste of rice flour and remaining fat. Leave in cold water. 5. Smear the rounds with the paste and roll. 6. Cut into 2.5 cm. (1") pieces. 7. Press each piece vertically. Roll into round shapes. 8. Fill with vegetable mixture and fold over, forming a semicircle. Press edges well. 9. Deep fry till golden brown. Drain.

FILLING

1. Boil potatoes and cauliflower and cut into small

pieces. 2. Boil and mash the peas. Chop onions. 3. Heat fat, brown onions, add the spices, vegetables, coriander leaves, green chillies and salt, sauté. 4. Cool and add lime juice.

Makes 15 puffs.

7. Green Peas Gungra

Filling		Chilli powder	½ tsp.
Green peas	225 gm.	Vinegar	1 tbsp.
Sweet potatoes	115 gm.	Oil	1 tbsp.
Green chillies	7—8 gm.	Covering	
Potatoes	115 gm.	Refined flour	225 gm.
Onions	500 gm.	Semolina	340 gm.
Coriander leaves	a few	Fat (creaming)	115 gm.
Salt	2 tsp.	Fat for dough	1 tbsp.
Sugar (optional)	1 tsp.	Oil to fry	
Turmeric	¼ tsp.		

1. Shell the green peas. 2. Peel and cut potatoes and sweet potatoes into small cubes. 3. Chop coriander leaves and green chillies. Heat one tbsp. oil. Sauté green peas. Add potatoes, sweet potatoes, onions, green chillies, dry spices and coriander leaves. 4. Add sufficient water to cook it dry. Add salt. 5. When nearly done, add vinegar and sugar and cook till dry. Remove from fire. 6. Mix semolina and one tsp. water. Rub in fat (one tbsp.). 7. Add enough water to make a fairly stiff dough. 8. Cream together 115 gm. of fat and the flour. 9. Keep on creaming till it forms a lump. 10. Keep the creamed mixture in water. 11. Roll out dough into thin chapaties. 12. Apply creamed mixture. Roll and cut into one inch slices. 13. Flatten out and roll into rounds about 7.5 cm. (3") in diameter. 14. Put in

prepared filling. Turn over. Seal the edges with water and decorate by fluting the edges. 15. Deep fry in fat till crisp and brown. Serve hot.

Makes 20 gungras.

8. Patrail

Colocasia leaves	1 dozen	Fat	30 gm.
(with black stems)		Turmeric	½ tsp.
Bengal gram flour	225 gm.	Coriander-cumin	
Whole wheat flour	40 gm.	powder	1 tsp.
Rice flour	20 gm.	Fenugreek seeds	5—6
Onions	200 gm.	Coconut	½ (115 gm.)
Green chillies	50 gm.	Tamarind	30 gm.
Coriander leaves	½ bunch	Vinegar	30 ml.
Ginger	2.5 cm. (1") piece	Jaggery	50 gm.
Garlic	5 flakes	Salt	2 tsp.
Cumin	½ tsp.	Sweet oil	2 tbsp.
Cooking banana	1	Oil to fry	

1. Grate, grind and soak coconut (set aside a tablespoonful for grinding) in 75 ml. of warm water, and extract milk. 2. Grind ginger, garlic, coriander leaves, half the onions, green chillies, remaining coconut, fenugreek, cumin, salt. 3. Soak tamarind in half a cup (about 75 ml.) of water. Add vinegar. 4. Peel and chop banana. 5. Chop and fry onions in fat. Sieve gram, rice and wheat flours and ground spices remaining fried onions, leftover fat, banana, turmeric, coriander-cumin powder, chilli powder and salt. 6. Mix tamarind pulp, jaggery and coconut milk and add to the mixture. 7. Add two tablespoons sweet oil. 8. Apply mixture on a colocasia leaf on the wrong side. Put another leaf on top and apply mixture again. Repeat till three leaves are used up in each group.

SNACKS 103

9. Turn in the two ends and roll tight. 10. Tie with thread and steam. Cut into slices. 11. Heat oil in a shallow frying pan and fry each piece. Serve hot.

Serves 10

9. Uppuma

Semolina	225 gm.	Bengal gram	15 gm.
Fat	30 gm.	Split black gram	15 gm.
Onion	55 gm.	Mustard seeds	3 gm.
Green chillies	5 gm.	Curry leaves	2 sprigs
Ginger	5 gm.	Water	
Coriander	a few sprigs	Lime	½
Peanuts	15 gm.	Salt	to taste

1. Heat fat. Add mustard seeds, peanuts, split black gram and Bengal gram and brown lightly. 2. Add chopped onion, ginger, green chillies and curry leaves. Sauté. 3. Add semolina. Roast till light brown. Add boiling water and salt. Allow to cook till dry. 4. Add a dash of lime juice and garnish with chopped coriander leaves. 5. Serve with or without chutney.

Serves 6.

N.B. After step 2, water in the proportion of 1:2 can be added and brought to boil and semolina sprinkled over and allowed to cook till dry, to obtain a slightly different flavour.

10. Sooji and Vegetable Uppuma

Semolina	450 gm.	Bengal gram	2 tsp.
Sprouted green gram (60 gm. before sprouting)	225 gm.	Split black gram	½ tsp.
		Mustard seeds	¼ tsp.
		Curry leaves	2 sprigs

SNACKS

Carrots	115 gm.	Asafoetida	a pinch
Green chillies	6 (20 gm.)	Salt	to taste
Ginger	5 gm.	Sugar	a pinch
Coriander leaves	1 bunch	Oil	150 ml.
Coconut	115 gm.	Lime	1

1. Prepare vegetables. Heat 100 ml. of oil. 2. Add Bengal gram, black gram, mustard seeds, curry leaves and asafoetida. 3. Add chopped carrots and sprouted gram. Sauté. 4. Add chopped green spices, ginger and salt and stir well. Add water to vegetables and bring to boil. 5. Meanwhile heat remaining oil and lightly fry semolina. 6. Add semolina to vegetables. 7. Stir and keep on a slow fire till cooked and dry. 8. Add lime juice, sugar and grated coconut. Mix well. 9. Remove from fire and serve hot.

Serves 6.

11. Idli

Rice	225 gm.	Fenugreek seeds	¼ tsp.
Split black gram	115 gm.	Salt	to taste

1. Wash and soak rice for about three hours. Strain and dry. 2. Grind coarsely in the grinder. 3. Soak gram for three to four hours and grind with fenugreek seeds till it is light and frothy. 4. Mix ground rice and ground gram and a little water and keep it overnight. 5. Add a pinch of salt and steam in idli steamer. Serve hot with coconut chutney.

Makes 20 idlis.

N.B. If parboiled rice is used the proportion of black gram to rice can be 1:3.

12. Dosa

Rice	300 gm.	Salt	5 gm.
Split black gram		Oil	30 gm.
(urad dal)	100 gm.		

1. Soak rice and gram separately. 2. Grind rice coarsely and gram to a smooth and fluffy consistency. 3. Mix together. Leave to ferment overnight. 4. Add salt and lukewarm water to form a pouring consistency. 5. Heat griddle. 6. Grease lightly with oil. 7. Pour a spoonful of mixture. Spread to form a round about 5-6" in diameter. 8. Cook for two minutes. Turn over. Cook for another minute or two. 9. Serve hot with coconut and roasted Bengal gram chutney.

Makes 12 dosas.

Coconut and Roasted Bengal Gram Chutney

Coconut	½	Ginger	5 gm.
Roasted chana dal		Salt	5 gm.
(bhuna chana)	50 gm.	Lime	1
Green chillies	10 gm.		

1. Grate coconut and grind to a coarse paste with roasted Bengal gram, green chillies and ginger. 2. Mix with salt and lime juice.

13. Rawa Dosa

Semolina	300 gm.	Buttermilk	120 ml.
Refined flour	30 gm.	Salt	to taste
Green chillies	5 gm.	Fat	30 gm.
Cumin	a pinch		

SNACKS

1. Chop green chillies fine. 2. Mix together semolina, flour, buttermilk and salt for the batter. 3. Let it stand for at least half an hour. 4. Heat a little fat. Add green chillies and cumin. 5. When cumin crackles add to batter. 6. Heat a griddle, smear surface with fat. 7. Pour a dsp. of batter to spread around. Pour a tsp. of fat around it and turn it over. 8. Remove when cooked. Serve hot with coconut chutney.
Serves 4.

14. Pesarattu

Green gram (whole)	115 gm.	Ginger	20 gm.
Green chillies	10 gm.	Salt	to taste
Onion	30 gm.	Fat	to shallow fry

1. Soak gram in water for about two hours. 2. Grind coarsely with onion; chop chillies fine and slice ginger. 3. Mix together ground gram, green chillies and salt. 4. Heat a frying pan. Grease it with a tsp. of fat. 5. Spread half the mixture in pan to form a round about 5 inches in diameter. Top with thin slices of ginger. 6. When one side is fried, turn over and fry the other. Add a little more fat if necessary.
Serves 4.

15. Khandvi

Buttermilk (thick)	150 ml. (1 cup)	Tempering Red chilli	1
Bengal gram flour	115 gm.	Asafoetida	a pinch
Water	150 ml.	Mustard seeds	½ tsp. (3 gm.)
Green chillies	2	Vegetable fat	10 gm.

Ginger	2.5 cm. (1") piece	Garnish	
Turmeric	½ tsp. (3 gm.)	Coconut	55 gm.
Salt	10 gm.	Coriander leaves	30 gm.

1. Mix together buttermilk, gram flour and water. 2. Grind chillies and ginger to a paste. 3. Mix all ingredients (except those for tempering and garnish) into a smooth solution and cook till water is almost absorbed and a soft dough consistency is obtained. 4. Grease plates with fat and spread mixture as thin as possible while still hot. 5. Cut into 5 cm. (2") strips. With a greased finger, roll up each strip. 6. Heat fat. Add whole red chilli, mustard seeds and asafoetida. As seeds crackle pour over prepared khandvi. 7. Garnish with grated coconut and chopped coriander leaves.

Serves 4.

16. Potato Kachories

Covering		Garam masala powder	a pinch
Refined flour	100 gm.	Lime	¼
Soda bicarb	a pinch	Mustard seeds	a few
Sour curd	20 gm.	Salt	to taste
Fat	20 gm.	Oil for tempering	5 gm.
Salt	to taste	Oil for frying (absorption)	30 ml.
Filling			
Potatoes	160 gm.	Imli Chutney	
Green peas	80 gm.	Tamarind	50 gm.
Green chillies	5 gm.	Jaggery	a little
Ginger	a small piece	Green chillies	2
Coriander leaves	a few	Chilli powder	a pinch
Turmeric	a small pinch	Salt	to taste

1. Sieve flour with salt. 2. Rub fat into flour. 3. Beat the curd with a little water and add to flour. 4. Add soda

bicarb dissolved in a little water. 5. Make a smooth dough and keep aside. 6. Boil potatoes in jackets. Peel and cut into cubes. 7. Boil peas and add to potatoes. 8. Remove seeds from green chillies and chop. Chop ginger and coriander leaves. 9. Add ginger, green chillies, coriander leaves and garam masala to potato and pea mixture. Mix well. 10. Heat oil. Add mustard seeds. As they crackle add turmeric and potato mixture. 11. Add lime juice and mix thoroughly. 12. Divide dough into equal portions. 13. Divide potato mixture into an equal number of portions. 14. Flatten dough between palms; fill centre with prepared stuffing, seal edges on top. 15. Deep fry till golden brown and serve piping hot with imli chutney. 16. For chutney, soak tamarind and extract juice. Mix all ingredients. Boil, strain and use.

Serves 4.

17. Cheese Toast

Cheese	30 gm.	Egg yolk	1
Bread	1 slice	Cayenne pepper	a pinch
Mustard	a large pinch	Salt and pepper	to taste
Baking powder	1/8 tsp.		

1. Mix together grated cheese, salt, pepper, mustard, baking powder and egg yolk. 2. Spread on bread. 3. Fry in deep fat.

Serves 1.

18. Pani Poori

Refined flour	55 gm.	Semolina	115 gm.
Split black gram flour	115 gm.	Cold water	to mix

SNACKS 109

Filling		Cooking salt	15 gm.
Sprouted green gram	55 gm.	Cumin	2 tsp.
Pani		Sweet cumin	15 gm.
Mint leaves	55 gm.	Cloves	4
Cold water	1.80 litres	Dry mango powder	115 gm.
Black pepper	15 gm.	Ginger	2.5 cm. (1") piece
Black salt	15 gm.		

1. Sieve the flours and semolina. Make a stiff dough. Knead well. 2. Make small balls. Roll into fairly thick poories. Spread on a moist cloth and cover with another moist cloth. 3. Deep fry in fat till light brown and crisp. 4. Boil the sprouted gram in salt water.

PANI
1. Wash mint leaves. Grind the mint leaves, cumin, sweet cumin, cloves and ginger. 2. Soak mango powder for an hour and sieve the pulp. 3. Powder salt and dissolve in cold water. 4. Mix the ground spices with pulp and salt water. 5. Strain and keep in an earthen pot.

TO SERVE
Make a hole in the poori and put in a few grains of sprouted gram. Dip the poori in the prepared liquid. Fill with pani and serve.

Serves 4-6.

19. Chiwda

Pressed rice	115 gm.	Chilli powder	½ tsp.
Cashewnuts	55 gm.	Chiwda masala powder	½ tsp.
Groundnuts	30 gm.	Curry leaves	1 tbsp.
Dry coconut (sliced)	15 gm.	Garlic	2 flakes

SNACKS

Sultanas	15 gm.	White gingelly	1 tsp.
Green chilli	1	Sugar (optional)	½ tsp.
Salt	to taste	Fresh oil to fry	
Turmeric	½ tsp.		

1. Heat oil. Fry pressed rice. Remove when it puffs up. Drain. 2. Mix turmeric with puffed rice. Set aside. 3. Fry cashewnuts till light brown. 4. Fry groundnuts, chilli, garlic, coconut, gingelly, sultanas, curry leaves, separately. Remove after frying and drain. 5. Add fried ingredients to fried pressed rice. Add chilli powder and chiwda masala powder. Mix well. 6. When the mixture is cold add broiled and powdered salt and sugar if desired.

Serves 4.

N.B. When frying pressed rice sprinkle small quantities of hot fat over it at intervals, or else it does not puff up properly.

CHIWDA MASALA

Dry mango powder	1 tsp.	*Cinnamon*	0.5 cm. (¼") piece
Cumin seeds	a pinch	*Omum*	a pinch
Fenugreek seeds	a pinch	*Red chilli*	1
Peppercorns	4		

1. Roast and powder all ingredients together.

20. Handwa

Rice flour (coarse)	1 kg.	*Bottle gourd*	500 gm.
Bengal gram flour	500 gm.	*Oil*	250 gm.
Black gram flour (coarse)	25 gm.	*Mustard seeds*	5 gm.
		Asafoetida	8 gm.

Masala

Cardamoms			
Cinnamon and			
Cloves	*8 gm.*	*Turmeric*	*8 gm.*
Green chillies	*25 gm.*	*Coriander seeds*	*40 gm.*
Onion	*50 gm.*	*Salt*	*to taste*

1. Grind masala to a fine paste. Mix all three flours with buttermilk, add more water to get a pouring consistency. 2. Add masala; peel and grate bottle gourd and add it to the mixture. 3. Heat oil in a thick pan. When hot, add mustard seeds and asafoetida. 4. When the mustard seeds crackle pour the oil on the mixture. 5. Mix well and keep it for about 12 hours to ferment. 6. Pour into shallow oven proof containers and bake the mixture for about 40 minutes. 7. Serve with green chutney.

Serves 6.

21. Paputtu (Coorg)

Broken rice	*100 gm.*	*Grated coconut*	*25 gm.*
(like large semolina)			*(½ teacup)*
	Milk	*180 ml.*	*(1 teacupful)*

1. Place rice in a shallow aluminium or enamel dish, about 0.5 cm. (1/4") deep. Add a pinch of salt. 2. Pour milk over. Sprinkle over with grated coconut. Steam. 3. Serve hot with meat curry.

Serves 4.

N.B. If desired, sugar to taste may be added by first dissolving it in milk. Milk and water may also be used in the proportion of 1:1.

PICKLES

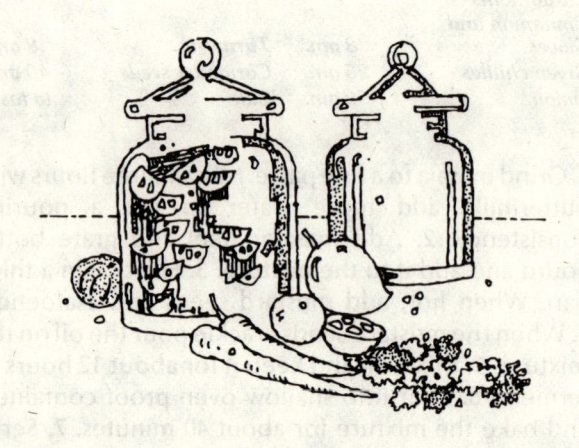

1. Gujarati Pickle

Raw mangoes (small)	*50*	*Salt*	*1.35 kg.*
Fenugreek seeds	*115 gm.*	*Turmeric*	*680 gm.*
Mustard seeds		*Asafoetida*	*2 tsp.*
(skin removed)	*100 gm.*	*Sesame oil*	*1 litre*
Chilli powder	*680 gm.*		

1. Slit mangoes into four. 2. Remove seed and fibre. 3. Stuff them with a mixture of salt and turmeric powder. Place in a glass jar and store for 48 hours. 4. Remove from the glass jar. 5. Dry for four to five hours, on a clean piece of cloth. 6. Mix together remaining ingredients, except oil, asafoetida and a tsp. of mustard. 7. Heat half the oil. Add asafoetida and one tsp. of mustard. When the seeds crackle, remove and pour over the mixed spices. Mix well. 8. Stuff the mangoes with the spices. Mix well. 9. Pack in a clean

glass jar. Set aside for three days. 10. Heat remaining oil. Cool and pour into the jar.

2. Avakkai

Medium sized mangoes	50	*Turmeric*	125 gm.
Salt	1 kg.	*Fenugreek seeds*	100 gm.
Mustard seeds	1 kg.	*Whole Bengal gram*	100 gm.
Red chillies	750 gm.	*Sesame oil*	1 litre

1. Cut mangoes into four with seeds, remove kernel. 2. Sun dry and powder separately mustard, chillies, turmeric and fenugreek seeds. Mix with salt immediately. 3. Mix all ingredients together. 4. Pack in a glass or earthenware jar. 5. Keep tightly covered for a week. 6. Mix well and use (if necessary add a little more oil).

3. Lime Pickle

Limes	25	*Salt*	225 gm.
Chilli powder	225 gm.	*Sesame oil*	1.25 litres
Turmeric powder	30 gm.	*Asafoetida*	
		(coarsely powdered)	2 tsp.

1. Wash and dry the limes. 2. Slit each into four half way down. 3. Fry asafoetida powder in a little oil. 4. Mix turmeric, chilli powder, asafoetida and salt. 5. Stuff the spices into the limes and leave them in an earthen jar for one day. 6. Heat oil in a deep frying pan to smoking point, cool, and pour over lime. 7. The pickle can be served after 15 days.

4. Karinellika

Amla (Indian gooseberry)	2 kg.	Pepper stems (tender)	20
Red chillies	100 gm.	Ginger	2.5 cm. (about 1" piece)
Red onions (small)	225 gm.	Salt	115 gm.
Garlic	50 gm.	Water	1 litre
Pepper	2 tbsp.	Sesame oil	60 ml.
Green chillies or kanthari	100 gm.	Curry leaves	1 sprig
Mustard seeds	1 tsp.		

1. Wash the gooseberries. Peel garlic, onions, ginger, etc. Slice ginger. Mix with broken red chillies and all the other ingredients except mustard seeds, pepper powder, curry leaves and oil. 2. Cover with water. Mix well and put into an earthenware fireproof pot. Cover with banana leaves tied round the opening. Boil for half an hour. 3. Remove and set aside. Reheat on slow fire every day for about 10-15 minutes. 4. Repeat for a week and ensure that by the end of the week the water has completely evaporated. 5. Heat oil. Add a tablespoons of mustard seeds, a sprig of curry leaves and two tablespoons pepper. When mustard seeds crackle, add the amla mixture. Mix well and bottle.

5. Brinjal Pickle

Brinjals	1 kg.	Mustard (whole)	20 gm.
Oil	250 ml.	Methi (whole)	15 gm.
Garlic	15 gm.	Sugar	50 gm.
Ginger, fresh	10 gm.	Cumin	10 gm.
Green chillies	40 gm.	Table salt	35 gm.
Chilli powder	40 gm.	White vinegar	150 ml.
Turmeric powder	20 gm.		

1. Wash and dry the brinjals, remove the stalks completely and cut into halves lengthwise. Slice each half into thin slices. Apply turmeric and set aside for a few minutes. Heat oil and fry till light brown, remove, add salt and sugar and keep aside. 2. Make a paste of green chillies, garlic and ginger, using white vinegar. 3. Pound methi, cumin and mustard into coarse powder. 4. Fry the paste in the remaining oil for two or three minutes, add pounded dry masala and finally the fried brinjals; mix well on slow fire. Finally add red chilli powder and remove from fire. Leave overnight. 5. Fill in jars, close tight, use after four or five days.

6. Mixed Vegetable Pickle

Cauliflower	1 kg.	Turmeric powder	15 gm.
Carrots	½ Kg.	White vinegar	400 ml.
Turnips	250 gm.	Mustard dal or powder	50 gm.
Fresh peas	500 gm.	Methi dal or powder	20 gm.
French beans	250 gm.	Red chilli powder	30—50 gm.
Green chillies	100 gm.	Asafoetida powder	10 gm.
Table salt	200 gm.	Refined oil (groundnut)	200 ml.

1. Wash thoroughly all the vegetables and dry in shade. 2. Dress each vegetable and cut into suitable sized pieces. (Total dressed weight of all the vegetables should be one kg.) 3. Mix together all the vegetables and add salt-turmeric mixture. 4. Cover with muslin cloth for four to five days. Mix well and leave for curing in the same jar or vessel for five to six days mixing occasionally (once in two days). 5. Heat the oil (not to smoking point). Add asafoetida, methi and mustard. Remove from burner. 6. Cool for five to six

minutes and finally add red chilli powder. 7. Mix well. Cool to room temperature and mix well with the pickled vegetables. Store for 10-12 days before use.

7 Watermelon Pickle

Thick watermelon rind	2 Kg.	Cinnamon	5 cm. (2") piece
Lime water, made with 2.4 litres of cold water and lime (calcium oxide)	1 tbsp.	Red chillies (whole)	10
		Vinegar	1 litre
		Water	1 litre
Peppercorns	2 tbsp.	Sugar	2 Kg.
Cloves	10		

1. Select thick rind from a firm, not over-ripe melon. To prepare, trim off the green skin and pink flesh. Weigh 2 Kg. of the remaining portion and cut into 2.5 cm. (about 1") pieces. 2. Soak for one hour in lime water. Drain, cover with fresh water and cook for 1½ hours or until tender. Add more water as needed. Drain. 3. Put the spices (except red chillies) in a muslin bag. Tie. Bring to boil the spices, vinegar, water and sugar. 4. Add watermelon rind and boil gently for two hours. Remove from fire. 5. Add whole chillies and let it hours. Remove from fire. 5. Add whole chillies and let it stand overnight. Remove spice bag. 6. Boil for one minute and pack into sterilised jars. Fill jars to the top with hot syrup and seal tight.

8. Chicken Pickle

Chicken	1 Kg.	Mustard seeds	30 gms.
Turmeric	30 gm.	Ginger	55 gm.
Garlic	30 gm.	Vinegar	120 ml.

Red Chillies	115 gm.	Mustard oil	(about) 500 ml.
Fenugreek seeds	15 gm.	Salt	115 gm.

1. Cut the chicken into small pieces. 2. Fry in mustard oil. 3. Grind all the spices separately in vinegar. 4. Take part of the mustard oil and fry turmeric, ginger, garlic, red chillies. 5. Add salt, fenugreek and mustard. Fry for two to three minutes. 6. Add fried chicken. Fry for another two to three minutes. Cool. 7. Add remaining mustard oil that has been previously heated and cooled.

9. Date Chutney

Dates	55 gm.	Garlic	5 gm.
Sugar	20 gm.	Vinegar	60 ml.
Red chillies	2	Salt	to taste
Ginger	5 gm.		

Remove seeds from chillies and soak in vinegar. Stone dates and grind. 3. Grind chillies, garlic and ginger using a little vinegar. 4. Make a syrup of the remaining vinegar and sugar. 5. Add ground spices and salt. Boil till syrup is thick. 6. Cool and add ground dates.

Serves 4.

INDEX OF RECIPES AND MAIN INGREDIENTS

Both recipes and main ingredients are listed here. Recipes are also listed under the main ingredients which are used in them. Recipes appear in bold type (as **Alu Chhole**).

The main ingredients are in roman (as Amla) and recipes listed under these are in italics as (*Karinellika*).

The numbers refer to page numbers.

Alu Chhole, 32
Amla
   Karinellika, 114
Assorted Pakoras, 98
Avakkai, 113

Ball Curry, 71
Balushai, 85
Beans Foogath, 35
Bengal Gram Flour
   Assorted Pakoras, 98
   Doodhi Kofta Curry, 42
   Handwa, 110
   Khandvi, 106
   Magaj, 91
   Mysore Pak, 94
   Patrail, 102

   Potato Bonda, 97
Bhaturas, 26
Bitter Gourd
   Pavakkai Varatharacha Curry, 40
Bibique, 95
Black Gram
   Makhani Dal, 33
Boiled Rice, 15
Boondi Ladoo, 91
Bottle Gourd
   Bottle Gourd Halwa, 110
   Doodhi Kofta Curry, 42
   Doodhi Pachadi, 44
   Handwa, 110
Brinjals
   Assorted Pakoras, 98

INDEX

Bhagare Baingan, 48
Brinjal Patiala, 47
Brinjal Pickle, 114
Vangi Bhath, 18
Buttermilk
  Khandvi, 106
  Moru Kulambu, 46
  Rawa Dosa, 105
Butter Tandoori Chicken, 82

Cabbage
  Cabbage Salad, 34
  Fried Rice, 22
  Shanghai Omelette, 23
Capsicum
  Stuffed Capsicum, 43
Carrots
  Carrot Halwa, 88
  Egg and Vegetable
    Moilee, 51
  Fried Rice, 22
  Mixed Vegetable
    Pickle, 115
  Shanghai Omelette, 23
  Vegetable Kababs, 43
Cashewnuts
  Bhagare Baingan, 48
  Cashew Potato Curry, 39
  Cashewnut Barfi, 90
  Chicken Khorma, 78
  Wheat Halwa, 89
Cauliflower
  Assorted Pakoras, 98
  Cauliflower Bhujia, 36
  Egg and Vegetable
    Moilee, 51
  Mixed Vegetable
    Pickle, 115
  Sikandari Gobhi, 44

Vegetable Kababs, 43
Vegetable Puffs, 100
Chapaties, 24
Cheese
  Cheese Toast, 108
  Stuffed Capsicum, 44
Chicken
  Buttered Tandoori
    Chicken, 82
  Chicken Cafreal, 82
  Chicken Chacouti, 77
  Chicken Curry, 77
  Chicken Fry Coorg, 81
  Chicken Khorma, 78
  Chicken Mulligutwanny
    Curry (Mild), 79
  Chicken Pickle, 116
  Chicken Shahjahani, 81
  Chicken Temperado, 80
  Fried Chicken, 79
  Kozhi Mulugu Veraval
    Chettinad, 83
  Rogini Chicken, 76
Chilli Powder
  Gujarati Pickle, 112
Chiroti, 86
Chiwda, 109
Cocktail Samosas With Liver Stuffing, 99
Coconut
  Bibique, 95
  Cashewnut Barfi, 90
  Chicken Chacouti, 77
  Chicken Khorma, 78
  Chicken Mulligutwanny
    Curry (Mild), 79
  Coconut and Roasted
    Bengal Gram
    Chutney, 105

INDEX

Coconut Barfi, 90
Egg and Potato Curry, 50
Egg and Vegetable Moilee, 51
Fish Curry (Green), 54
Fish Moilee, 55
Ginger Curry, 47
Mango/Green Tomato Pachhadi, 45
Meat and Coconut Fry, 69
Moru Kulambu, 46
Patrani Machhi, 56
Pavakkai Varatharacha Curry, 40
Prawn Caldeen, 60
Cocum
Garlic Kadhi, 32
Colocasia Leaves
Patrail, 102
Cottage Cheese
Palak Panir, 38
Panir Makhani, 38
Curd
Chicken Khorma, 78
Doodhi Pachadi, 45
Grilled Spare Ribs, 73
Moghlai Biryani, 20
Onion Raita, 45
Prawn Nissa, 60
Rogini Chicken, 76
Salli Ka Gosht, 70
Sikandari Gobhi, 44

Dal, 29
Date And Tamarind Chutney, 98
Date Chutney, 117
Doodh Kamal, 88
Doodhi Kofta Curry, 42
Doodhi Pachadi, 44
Dosa, 105
Duck Roast, 84

Eggs
Egg and Potato Curry, 50
Egg and Vegetable Moilee, 51
Egg Rice, 17
Shanghai Omelette, 23
Egg White
Thali Sweet, 94
Egg Yolk
Bibique, 95

Falooda, 87
French Beans
Beans Foogath, 35
Mixed Vegetable Pickle, 115
Vegetable Kababs, 43
Fish
Fish Curry (Green), 54
Fish Curry (Madras), 58
Fish Fry (Goan), 54
Fish Fry (Punjabi), 53
Fish in Sauce, 56
Fish Moilee, 55
Lobster Masala, 61
Machlisalan (Punjabi), 57
Machi Koliwada, 55
Malayalee Fish Curry, 58
Patrani Machhi, 56
Prawn Caldeen, 60
Prawns in Garlic Chilli Sauce, 59
Prawn Nissa, 60

INDEX

Fried Chicken, 79
Fried Lady's Fingers, 35

Garlic Kadhi, 32
Ginger Curry, 47
Grams:
Gram Flour
  Boondi Ladoo, 91
Split Bengal Gram
  Saag Bhaji, 30
  Vangibhat, 18
  Vegetable Kababs, 43
Split Black Gram
  Dosa, 105
  Idli, 104
  Pani Puri, 108
  Vangi Bhath, 18
Split Green Gram
  Moong Dal Khichdi, 16
Sprouted Green Gram
  Sooji and Vegetable Uppuma, 103
Green Gram
  Pesarattu, 106
Split Red Gram
  Dal, 29
  Masala Vada, 96
  Rasam,
  Tur Dal and Vegetable Sorak, 30
Green Curry (Meat/Chicken/Liver), **64**
Green Peas Gungra, 101
Grilled Spare Ribs, 73
Gulab Jamun, 92
Gujarati Pickle, 112

Handwa, 110

Hyderabadi Kheema, 72

Idli, 104

Jaggery
  Peanut Chikki, 92

Karinellika, 114
Khandvi, 106

Lady's Fingers
  Assorted Pakoras, 98
  Fried Lady's Fingers, 35
  Prawn Caldeen, 60
Lamb
  Raan-E-Noorjahan, 66
  Safed Mas, 68
Leeks
  Fried Rice, 22
  Shanghai Omelette, 23
Lentils
  Tomato Mahasha, 36
Lime Pickle, 113
Lobster Masala, 61

Machlisalan (Punjabi), **57**
Magaj, 91
Makhani Dal, 33
Malayalee Fish Curry, 58
Mangoes
  Avakkai, 113
  Mango Pachhadi, 45
Masala Trotters, 73
Masala Vada, 96
Mawa
  Coconut Barfi, 90
  Gulab Jamun, 92

122 INDEX

Magaj, 91
Meat And Coconut Fry, 69
Methi Ki Roti, 27
Milk
  Bottle Gourd Halwa, 89
  Carrot Halwa, 88
  Doodh Kamal, 88
  Falooda, 87
  Paputtu, 111
  Phirnee, 87
  Semiya Payasam, 86
  Shahi Tukra, 92
  Shrikhand, 93
Minced Meat
  Kheema Kaleji, 74
Mixed Vegetable Pickle, 115
Moghlai Biryani, 20
Moghlai Parathas, 25
Moong Dal Khichdi, 16
Moru Kulambu, 46
Mutton
  Ball Curry (Malabar), 71
  Country Captain, 66
  Green Curry (Mutton), 64
  Hyderabadi Kheema, 72
  Moghlai Biryani, 20
  Meat and Coconut Fry, 69
  Mutton Curry (Mild), 67
  Mutton Baffat, 62
  Mutton Bhopla, 65
  Mutton Jhal Faraizi, 70
  Mutton Khorma, 63
  Roganjosh, 68
  Salli Ka Gosht, 70
  Shami Kababs, 72
  Shahi Khorma, 64
  Qorma Biryani, 21
  Yakhni Pulao, 19
Mysore Pak, 94

Onions
  Alu Chhole, 32
  Assorted Pakoras, 98
  Cabbage Salad, 34
  Chicken Khorma, 78
  Egg and Potato Curry, 50
  Egg and Vegetable Moilee, 51
  Fried Rice, 22
  Green Pea Gungra, 101
  Mutton Jhal Faraizi, 70
  Onion Cuchumber, 34
  Onion Raita, 45
  Samosas, 99
  Shanghai Omelette, 23
  Tomato Mahasha, 36-7
  Vegetable Kababs, 43

Pal Appam, 26
Palak Panir, 38
Pani Puri, 108
Panir Makhani, 38
Paputtu (Coorg), 111
Patrail, 102
Patrani Machhi, 56
Pavakkai Varatha Vacha Curry, 40
Peanut Chikki, 92
Peas
  Green Peas Gungra, 101
  Mixed Vegetable Pickle, 115
  Shuktoni, 37
Pesarattu, 106
Phirnee, 87
Pork
  Grilled Spare Ribs, 73
Potatoes
  Alu Bhurta, 41

Alu Chhole, 32
Assorted Pakoras, 98
Bhaturas, 26
Cashew Potato Curry, 39
Egg and Potato Curry, 50
*Egg and Vegetable
  Moilee*, 51
Mutton Jhal Faraizi, 70
Potato Bonda, 97
Potato Kachories, 107
Samosas, 99
Shuktoni, 37
Stuffed Capsicum, 43
Stuffed Parathas, 24
Til Alu Dum, 41
Vegetable Kababs, 43
Vegetable Puffs, 100
Prawns
  Fried Rice, 22
  Masala Vada, 96
  Prawn Caldeen, 60
  *Prawns in Garlic Chilli
    Sauce*, 59
  Prawn Nissa, 60
  Shanghai Omelette, 23
Pumpkin
  Assorted Pakoras, 98
  Mutton Bhopla, 65

Qorma Biryani, 21

Raan-E-Noorjahan, 66
Rasam, 31
Rawa Dosa, 105
Refined Flour
  Balushai, 85
  Bhaturas, 26
  Chiroti, 86

Green Pea Gungra, 101
Moghlai Parathas, 25
Pani Puri, 108
Potato Kachories, 107
Samosas, 99
Vegetable Puffs, 100
Rice
  Boiled Rice, 15
  Dosa, 105
  Egg Rice, 17
  Fried Rice, 22
  Idli, 104
  Moghlai Biryani, 20
  Moong Dal Khichdi, 16
  Qorma Biryani, 21
  Til Rice, 17
  Vangi Bhath, 18
  Vegetable Pulao, 18
  Yakhni Pulao, 19
  Yellow Rice, 16
Rice Flour
  Chiroti, 86
  Handwa, 110
  Pal Appam, 26
  Phirnee, 87
Roganjosh, 68
Rogini Chicken, 76
Rose Syrup
  Falooda, 87

Saag Bhaji, 30
Safed Mas, 68
Salli Ka Gosht, 70
Samosas, 99
Semiya Payasam, 86
Semolina
  Green Pea Gungra, 101
  Pal Appam, 26
  Pani Puri, 109

INDEX

Rawa Dosa, 105
Sooji and Vegetable Uppuma, 103
Thali Sweet, 94
Uppuma, 103
Shahi Khorma, 64
Shahi Tukra, 92
Shami Kababs, 72
Shrikhand, 93
Shuktoni, 37
Sikandari Gobhi, 44
Sooji And Vegetable Uppuma, 103
Spinach
Palak Panir, 38
Saag Bhaji, 30
Spinach Puris, 27
Stuffed Capsicum, 43
Stuffed Parathas, 24

Tamarind
Date and Tamarind Chutney, 98
Tamarind Chutney, 97
Thali Sweet, 94
Til Alu Dum, 41
Til Rice, 17
Tomatoes
Alu Chhole, 32
Doodhi Kofta Curry, 42
Egg and Vegetable Moilee, 51
Green Tomato Pachhadi, 45

Hyderabadi Kheema, 72
Tomato Chilli Chutney, 98
Tomato Mahasha, 36-37
Tomato Puree
Panir Makhani, 38
Trotters
Masala Trotters, 73
Tur Dal And Vegetable Sorak, 30
Turnips
Mixed Vegetable Pickle, 115

Uppuma, 103

Vangi Bhath, 18
Vegetable Fried Rice, 22
Vegetable Kababs, 43
Vegetable Puffs, 100
Vegetable Pulao, 18
Vermicelli
Semiya Payasam, 86

Watermelon Pickle, 116
Whole Wheat Flour
Chapaties, 24
Methi Ki Roti, 27
Spinach Puris, 27
Stuffed Parathas, 24
Wheat Halwa, 89

Yellow Rice, 16
Yakhni Pulao, 19